The EQ Educator:

Integrating
SOCIAL EMOTIONAL
LEARNING
into Schools

Edited by Lorea Martinez, Ph.D.
and Susan Stillman, Ed.D.
Six Seconds Global Office

sixseconds
THE EMOTIONAL INTELLIGENCE NETWORK

Copyright ©2018, Six Seconds
Editors: Lorea Martinez, Ph.D. and Susan Stillman, Ed.D.
Book Design: Saravanan Ponnaiyan
ISBN: 978-1-935667-35-3
Printed in the USA

Library of Congress Cataloging-in-Publication Data
Martinez, Lorea (editor) and Stillman, Susan (editor)
The EQ Educator: Integrating Social Emotional Learning into Schools
1. Education. 2 Psychology

Six Seconds

Mail: PO Box 1985, Freedom, CA 95019
Web: www.6seconds.org
Email: staff@6seconds.org
Phone: (831) 763-1800

Contents

Introduction

Welcome! This book is written to help you – teachers, counselors, administrators in schools, and faculty in higher education integrate Emotional Intelligence (EQ) and Social Emotional Learning (SEL) into your practice and organization. This book has been used as required reading in higher education courses and in professional development, supporting meaningful teaching and learning. We hope all educators may benefit from knowing about the exciting innovations and science in SEL and their practical applications.

In this book, we have prepared a collection of great articles and other resources that will help you deepen your understanding of EQ and the many ways it can help you as educators, your colleagues, and the students that you serve.

First, we'd like to tell you just a little about EQ and Six Seconds.

What is EQ?

Emotional intelligence means being smarter with feelings. It's about using both are heads and our hearts to make optimal decisions and be more effective in our lives and work. EQ helps us all be more aware, more intentional, and more purposeful. Josh Freedman, CEO of Six Seconds, wrote that "Learning is both emotional and rational. So educators need to be good at both . . . Learning is a risk. That is why learners need courage and safety." EQ can help you develop your own social and emotional competencies and create the best possible conditions for learning in your classroom.

What is Six Seconds?

Six Seconds is a global community of change-makers contributing to a world of insight, connection, and purpose.

We think the world would be a better place if a billion people were practicing the skills of emotional intelligence. So, we research and share scientific, global, transformational tools and methods to support that goal.

As you start your EQ journey, we invite you to join us in this vision.

In this reader, you'll find some of our favorite articles from our Six Seconds' website and from SEL consultant, Dr. Lorea Martinez' blog. Many additional powerful articles are available on the Six Seconds website: 6seconds.org and additional resources on EQ.org, including SEL sample lessons. We encourage you to explore these great resources and share them with your colleagues.

> *Emotional intelligence means being smarter with feelings.*

EQ Development

At Six Seconds, we believe emotions are valuable signals that help us survive and thrive. When we learn how to use them, emotions help us make more effective decisions, connect with others, find and follow purpose — and lead a more whole-hearted life.

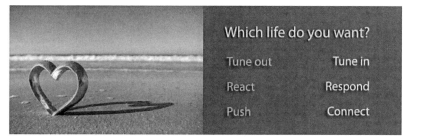

Which life do you want?

Tune out	Tune in
React	Respond
Push	Connect

In simple terms, "emotional intelligence" just means being smarter with feelings. It's about putting together the rational and emotional so you can move forward effectively. Emotions are part of human biology; they are chemicals that help regulate our minds and bodies, assisting us to cope with the complexities of making decisions, interacting with people, and finding our way through life. We feel emotions to help us pay attention and to focus our attention. While sometimes they're confusing, emotions are part of us, so we might as well learn to use them well.

In the next pages, you will have an opportunity to learn how EQ can help teachers and other adults working with children and youth and discover the value of EQ for students.

Social Emotional Learning (SEL) is most effective when it begins from the inside out.

1. EQ for Teachers and Administrators

EQ competencies are important for student achievement, motivation, and school engagement. They are also critical ingredients for supportive teacher-student relationships, for classroom management, and as a solution to teacher burnout (Jennings & Greenberg, 2009; Jones, Bouffard, & Weissbourd, 2013).

Social Emotional Learning (SEL) is most effective when it begins "from the inside out," with teachers deepening their own competencies, forming meaningful quality relationships with students and modeling SEL behaviors and attitudes.

According to Shriver and Buffett (2015), the relationship between teacher and student is strengthened when teachers focus on their own SEL skills. The Missing Piece Report warns that to the extent that we ignore SEL, we are disengaging both teachers and students from learning and from contributing to a thriving learning community (Bridgeland, Bruce, & Hariharan, 2013).

In the next pages, you will read about the Six Seconds Model of Emotional Intelligence. If you would like to know how you are putting your EQ into practice, we recommend the SEI – Six Seconds Emotional Intelligence Assessment. This tool assesses competence and offers a practical roadmap for development. You can read more about this powerful tool in this chapter.

1.1 The Six Seconds Model

The Six Seconds model turns EQ theory into practice for your personal and professional life.

Emotional intelligence is the capacity to blend thinking and feeling to make optimal decisions — which is key to having a successful relationship with yourself and others. To provide a practical and simple way to learn and practice emotional intelligence, Six Seconds developed a three-part model in 1997 as a process – an action plan for using emotional intelligence in daily life.

This model of EQ-in-Action begins with **three important pursuits:** to become more aware (noticing what you do), more intentional (doing what you mean), and more purposeful (doing it for a reason).

Know Yourself

Clearly seeing what you feel and do. Emotions are data, and these competencies allow you to accurately collect that information.

Choose Yourself

Doing what you mean to do. Instead of reacting "on autopilot," these competencies allow you to proactively respond.

Give Yourself

Doing it for a reason. These competencies allow you to put your vision and mission into your daily action so you lead "on purpose" and with full integrity.

> 66
>
> *Learnable, measurable, scientifically validated*
> *competencies*
>
> 99

Know Yourself gives you the "**what**" – when you Know Yourself, you know your strengths and challenges, you know what you are doing, what you want, and what to change.

Choose Yourself provides the "**how**" – it shows you how to take action, how to influence yourself and others, how to "operationalize" these concepts.

Give Yourself delivers the "**why**" – when you Give Yourself you are clear and full of energy so you stay focused on why to respond a certain way, why to move in a new direction, and why others, like your colleagues or your students, should come on board.

You'll notice we present the model in a CIRCLE – it's not a list, it's a process! The process works when you spin it, like a propeller moving a ship. As you move through these three pursuits you gain positive momentum!

"Under" the three pursuits live eight specific, learnable, measurable competencies. They're measured through the Six Seconds Emotional Intelligence Assessment – or SEI. Here are the eight competencies – with definitions below:

Know Yourself

1. Enhance Emotional Literacy

DEFINITION:

Accurately identifying and understanding feelings.

Importance: Emotions are chemicals, a form of neurotransmitter, that provide data about yourself and others; emotions are a feedback system delivering information that drives behavior and decisions. Emotional literacy is the capacity to access and interpret that data.

Emotional literacy helps you notice, name, and understand feelings. This provides critical information about you and about others, which gives you insight into the core drivers of behavior. This understanding is also key to managing your reactions.

> *The human brain is wired to form and follow neural pathways.*

2. Recognize Patterns

DEFINITION:

Acknowledging frequently recurring reactions and behaviors.

Importance: Sometimes people assess new situations and respond carefully and thoughtfully, but frequently they run on autopilot, reacting unconsciously based on habit. In part, it's because the human brain is wired to form and follow neural pathways. Left unconscious, these patterns can inhibit optimal performance because they are a generalized response rather than one carefully tailored to the current situation.

Recognizing Patterns helps you track and monitor your reactions – which is an essential step to managing them. Recognizing your own patterns will also help you see others' – which will be invaluable in coaching and supporting others so they get off of autopilot as well.

Choose Yourself

3. Apply Consequential Thinking

DEFINITION:

Evaluating the costs and benefits of your choices.

Importance: This skill helps you assess your decisions and their effects. It is key to managing your impulses and acting intentionally (rather than reacting). It's a process of analyzing and reflecting, using both thoughts and feelings, to identify a response that is optimal for you and others.

This competence is critical for making a strategic plan that accounts for the human dynamics – and for managing your own behavior as you execute that plan.

4. Navigate Emotions

DEFINITION:

Assessing, harnessing, and transforming emotions as a strategic resource.

Importance: People are often told to control their emotions, to suppress feelings like anger, joy, or fear, and eliminate them from the decision-making process. However, feelings provide insight and energy; they drive decision-making and behavior – without emotion, people literally cannot make decisions.

So rather than ignoring feelings or controlling them through sheer force of will, this competence lets you manage emotions, gain valuable insight from them, and then transform them so you create feelings that are helpful to you and others.

5. Engage Intrinsic Motivation

DEFINITION:

Gaining energy from personal values and commitments vs. being driven by external forces.

Importance: People who require external reinforcement to be motivated are always at the mercy of others' approval or reward system. This ultimately reduces self-efficacy.

Engaging Intrinsic Motivation helps you develop and use lasting inner drivers. This allows you to stand up, challenge the status quo, take risks, and persevere when the going is tough – and it helps you inspire that in others.

> *An optimistic outlook increases the pool of choices and the opportunity for success.*

6. Exercise Optimism

DEFINITION:

Taking a proactive perspective of hope and possibility.

Importance: This learned way of thinking + feeling gives you ownership of your decisions and outcomes. Everyone uses both optimistic and pessimistic styles of feeling + thinking; some tend to use one more often.

An optimistic outlook increases the pool of choices and the opportunity for success. This provides a solution-oriented approach, helps you innovate, and allows you to engage others' positive energy. Optimism helps you see beyond the present and take ownership of the future.

Give Yourself

7. Increase Empathy

DEFINITION:

Recognizing and appropriately responding to others' emotions

Importance: Empathy is a nonjudgmental openness to others' feelings and experiences that builds connection and awareness. It starts by noticing both the pleasant and unpleasant feelings and genuinely caring what the other person is experiencing. The next steps include listening, sharing, and responding in a way that shows your concern.

Empathy is key to understanding others and forming enduring and trusting relationships. It ensures you take other people into account in your decision-making and gives them a rock-solid assurance that you are on the same team.

> *A Noble Goal provides clarity and the commitment & energy to make more careful choices*

8. Pursue Noble Goals

DEFINITION:

Connecting your daily choices with your overarching sense of purpose.

Importance: Noble Goals activate all of the other competencies in the Six Seconds Model. When people examine their personal vision, mission, and legacy, and use that conviction to set their goals and objectives, emotional intelligence gains relevance and power.

When you are clear about your Noble Goal, you feel compelled to pay fierce attention to your daily choices to ensure that you are not undermining your life's purpose. Pursuing a Noble Goal facilitates integrity and ethical behavior, which helps you maintain focus, inspire others, and access your full power and potential.

1.2 The SEI, Assessment of Emotional Intelligence

The SEI, or Six Seconds Emotional Intelligence Assessment is a well validated, effective tool that measures EQ and equips people with a framework for putting emotional intelligence into action.

Where several other EQ tools provide meaningful feedback, the SEI is unique because it's not JUST feedback, it delivers a process framework that equips people to actually USE emotional intelligence The SEI also links EQ to real life; it includes two questionnaires, an assessment of current "success factors" (e.g., effectiveness and relationships) and the EQ measure; this puts EQ in the context of important work & life outcomes, providing the "so what?" to make EQ relevant. Take a look at the following example:

SEI Report Sample

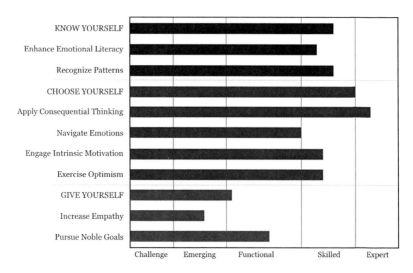

What would you say are this person's strengths? And his/her growth areas? How could this person improve an area of vulnerability by using a strength? If this person were a teacher, what would be some challenges s/he might encounter?

Many educators find the SEI data, and the individual debrief that goes with it, an invaluable tool for deepening their own EQ skills and understanding their interactions with others, including their families, friends, instructors, colleagues, and students.

For more information about this practical tool, visit http://www.6seconds.org/tools/sei/

> 66
> *SEI provides feedback to make emotional intelligence relevant and actionable.*
> 99

1.3 An EQ Action Plan

The Situation. What is it you want to change or make better in yourself and/or in your classroom? What feelings are involved?

The Opportunity. Where can you influence this problem? What feelings would be helpful? (Consider your existing systems, structures, relationships.)

The Plan. What EQ competencies can you apply to address the problem? What are the next steps for you and/or your students? (Don't forget to consider how you'll make the emotional shifts - what feeling-ripples do you want to send?)

The Result. How will success look and feel? How will you know you've created the desired results? What will it mean for you and/or your classroom? (What are some key metrics or milestones?)

1.4 Navigate Emotions in the Six Seconds Model

By Michael Miller

Emotional intelligence is the capacity to blend thinking and feeling to make optimal decisions — which is key to having a successful relationship with yourself and others . . .

– Joshua Freedman

Navigate Emotions Definition: Assessing, harnessing, and transforming emotions as a strategic resource.

Importance: By learning to transform emotions as a strategic resource, we can become more aware, balanced, and purposeful. Instead of thinking of emotions as something bad that we have to suppress, we can begin to treat all of our emotions, even challenging ones like anger, as invaluable data helping us to be our best selves. We can turn something often seen as an adversary and make it into an ally.

Example: Imagine you are stuck in traffic, running late, and feeling frustrated. Someone is trying to get over into your lane, and you catch yourself mumbling something negative about them. Then you say to yourself, "It's not his fault. I am frustrated because I am running late and stuck in traffic." And oddly, this simple admission makes you feel a lot better. By saying to yourself what you are feeling, you have lessened the power of the emotion and brought the emotional and cognitive together. Instead of admonishing yourself for feeling frustrated, you simply acknowledge the emotion, and, as a result, make it your ally.

Navigating emotions helps you take ownership of your life. By fully integrating your thinking and feeling, you are able to make optimal decisions – which is key to reaching your goals and strengthening your relationship with self and others.

The Components of Navigate Emotions

Assess: The first step of navigating emotions is to assess what you are feeling. Identifying or naming emotions, to yourself or aloud, can add some needed clarity to this step.

Harness: Recognize that there are not good or bad emotions: emotions are data. Taking the step back from "I am frustrated..." to "I am feeling frustrated..." helps provide space and lessens the power of the emotion. Recognize that the emotion is temporary and is providing you valuable information about yourself and the world.

Transform: The emotion, however difficult, is now your ally. It has sent you data about the world, which you have accepted and can now use to be more aware and purposeful.

To read more about Six Seconds EQ competencies, go to www.6seconds.org/articles

> 66
>
> *Instead of thinking of emotions as something bad that we have to suppress, we can begin to treat all of our emotions, even challenging ones like anger, as invaluable data.*
>
> 99

1.5 Six Seconds Research: Improving School Leaders' Effectiveness Through EQ

By Lorea Martinez, Ph.D.

What would happen at your school if you had leaders with high emotional intelligence?

The increased focus on improving student achievement has created the expectation that principals excel in many roles: instructional leaders, community builders, program designers, and advocates for all children. Unfortunately, agreement does not exist as to the most effective approaches to developing transformational school administrators. What skills do principals need in order to be effective leaders?

The development of leaders' Emotional Intelligence (EQ) is widely accepted as essential to effective performance in the corporate arena, but to educators, the concept of EQ within school leadership is still new. In fact, the development of social, emotional and cognitive skills has been called the "missing link" in school leaders' preparation (Patti, Senge, Madrazo, & Stern, 2015).

Six Seconds' researchers Lorea Martinez, SEL Consultant; Susan Stillman, Director of Education; Paul Stillman, Director of Organizational Vitality; and Tom Procicchiani, Research and Design Engineer, sought to address this gap in the literature by studying how principals engage EQ to support their leadership practices and exploring the factors that enable or hinder principals' use of their EQ skills.

Research to Support Principals' Leadership Effectiveness

On May 1st, 2017, Dr. Lorea Martinez presented this research at the 2017 Annual Conference of the American Education Research Association (AERA) in San Antonio, Texas, during the roundtable "School Leaders Ready to Lead: Developing the Social and Emotional Skills of School Administrators."

Six Seconds' researchers studied a group of principals in an urban school district in California during one school year. During the study, the researchers administered and debriefed participants on two Six Seconds measurement tools, the SEI and the Leadership Vital Signs, and conducted 4 interventions and 4 focus groups to explore the use of EQ by these principals and identify the factors at the school level that enabled or hindered their use of EQ skills.

The Research Journey

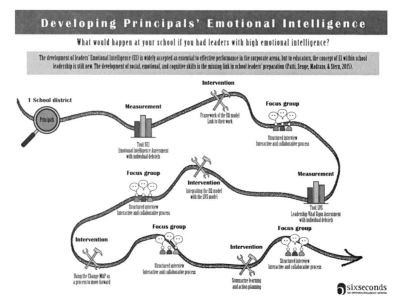

Key Findings in Principals' Use of EQ

The research revealed themes pertinent to those supporting leadership effectiveness in educational settings:

1. What role do emotions play in principals' understanding of their leadership skills?

At the beginning of the study, 75% of principals were focused on rational data, while 25% were focused on emotional information. Through the interventions and focus groups, principals started harnessing emotions as a strategic resource. Principals also began to recognize the power of emotions to solve problems and create opportunities. They started a process of opening up, by listening and connecting, accepting vulnerability, and empowering others around them.

> 66
>
> *It's helping me with knowing my own emotions, which makes me more effective in working with other people at the site – parents, teachers and children.*
>
> 99

2. How do principals use emotional intelligence to support their leadership at school?

Principals in this study had practical drive, with problem solving and commitment being their top talents. These school leaders found EQ helpful in envisioning their schools. They were able to connect with their own purpose through self-reflection and communicate a vision with shared language. Through this study, principals started using EQ data to gain concrete tools. They expressed being able to use empathy to get others on board and identified an increased sense of confidence in shared ownership with their staff.

> *[EQ means] allowing myself not always to be the answer.*

3. What factors at the school level enable or hinder the use of emotional intelligence by principals?

Engaging Intrinsic Motivation and Pursuing a Noble Goal (two key competencies in the Six Seconds EQ model) were these school leaders' top self-identified skills, while Enhancing Emotional Literacy and Increasing Empathy were the lowest. Principals expressed being challenged by the practical demands of the job and the experience of powerful emotions. They identified EQ as essential to enable coping and achieving wellbeing and placed a high value on relationships to enact meaning for themselves and others.

> *Leveraging strengths in motivation and optimism to increase empathy and improve consequential thinking.*

In summary, this study illustrates how EQ skill acquisition is an important component in the development of effective school leaders. EQ should be embedded in pre-service and professional development for school leaders. In addition, increased opportunities at the district level should be provided so principals can focus on EQ and leadership development.

Next Step

If you are a leader in an educational organization ready to improve your leadership, contact us for support and strategies.

2. EQ for Students

Successful students develop outcomes associated with SEL competencies, such as resilience, tenacity, perseverance, and positive academic mindsets. Researchers at Six Seconds have shown that students who develop their SEL competencies will have higher scores for good health, relationship quality, personal achievement, life satisfaction, and self- efficacy (Jensen, Fieldeldey-van Dijk, & Freedman, 2012).

Students with SEL skills also exhibit broader social emotional competencies such as interacting with diverse individuals and groups in socially skilled and respectful ways. They also contribute responsibly to their family, school, and community. While the emphasis historically has been on student achievement, experts in SEL are emphasizing the school as learning organization (Senge et al., 2000) and the importance of all stakeholders becoming socially and emotionally adept. As Brackett (2015) has said, "everyone with a face" needs to be invested in an SEL school.

The following articles will help you identify the role that emotions play in learning and how to support students in decoding and navigating their emotions. Once you have read the articles, complete the reflection page.

2.1 *Emotions and Learning*

How emotions affect learning, part 1
By Lorea Martinez, Ph.D.

Emotions are an important part of human life. We experience emotions all the time, but we rarely pause to reflect on what emotions are and how they affect learning. Emotions drive attention; they influence our ability to process information and to understand what we encounter. They can energize our thinking or distract us from our goals. Part 1 of this post is focused on the concept of emotion. In part 2, we'll discuss how emotions affect learning.

Emotions are complex states of mind and body, generally activated by an event, which is known as *stimulus*. Events can be external (you received great news from a friend) or internal (you have a toothache); they can be real or also imagined (you get excited when thinking about an upcoming party).

Once a stimulus has been generated, there is a process to *appraise* (Lazarus, 1991) it. This process is automatic and determines if the event is perceived as positive or negative, which will produce an emotional response. For example, if I am riding my bike and a car gets too close, I appraise that I am in danger, and this activates my emotional response.

We can identify 3 different emotional responses (Bisquerra, 2009):

Physiological: involuntary responses such as sweat, dry mouth, heavy breathing, or rapid heartbeat.

Behavioral: Facial expressions, body language, or tone of voice.

Cognitive: This is the subjective experience of the emotion. It allows us to become aware and name our emotions. Having the language to name and describe our emotions is key to identify "what's happening."

Emotions drive us to take action, either by facing the event or by moving away from the situation that produced them. This predisposition to action is also known as *fight or flight response,* which reflects the two basic behaviors that ensure survival. Although emotions drive us to take action, it doesn't necessarily mean that the action needs to occur. For example, if we feel offended by someone's comment, we might feel the urge to respond aggressively. **This predisposition to action can be regulated with some training; this is where teaching SEL comes into place.**

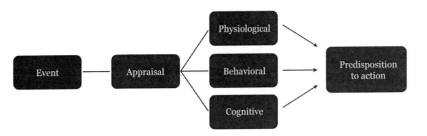

Model of emotion (Bisquerra, 2009)

Developing students' social and emotional competencies means helping students be aware of their emotions, so they can regulate them and avoid impulsive reactions. A few suggestions to develop your students' self-awareness and self-management:

- Implement Quiet Time in your classroom. Quiet Time provides students with a regular quiet, peaceful, restful period to meditate, do sustained silent reading or free drawing. It helps students de-stress and re-focus for better learning.

- Develop students' emotional literacy by discussing different emotions, building an emotion thermometer or identifying character emotions in the books you're reading with students.

- Help students reframe the way they think about their emotions and themselves.

Today, we explored how emotions are activated by events that we appraise as positive or negative, generating a physiological, behavioral and cognitive response and preparing us to take action. Implementing quiet time, discussing emotions in the classroom, and helping students reframe the way they think about what they feel are some ways to develop students' self-awareness, so they can better regulate their behaviors.

Originally published in Social Emotional Learning and the Common Core blog by Lorea Martinez, Ph.D.

How emotions affect learning, part 2

By Lorea Martinez, Ph.D.

In an earlier post, I discussed the concept of emotion and offered a few suggestions to build self-awareness and self-management in your students. After reading the blog, did you start identifying your different emotional responses during the day? Did you find yourself paying more attention to how your emotions predispose you to act? Understanding how emotions *work* is key to build our awareness! Today, we'll explore how emotions affect learning.

Students bring to the classroom emotions from life outside of school; they might be dealing with an ongoing stressful situation at home, like a divorce or a parent losing their job, or maybe something more momentary, like an argument with a sibling. If students didn't have a chance to manage their emotions before getting to school, they will need your support to cool off and re-focus before they can move on with their day.

In addition, students also experience emotions that originate in the classroom and that are especially relevant for students' learning (Pekrun, 2014):

Topic emotions pertain to the topics/subjects presented in class. Students might feel excited about a new art class, disgusted with certain lab experiments, or saddened by the fate of a character in a novel.

Social emotions relate to teachers and classmates, as students (and teachers) work together and interact in the classroom. Compassion, envy, sympathy, anger, or social anxiety can be present at different times during the day with any and all of our students.

As a teacher, it might be difficult to respond to your students' emotions at all times, while you manage the classroom and attend to academic content. However, there are things you can do to incorporate students' emotions when you are planning and also during class.

Offer a variety of tasks and activities, so students can feel successful during your class/period, and **combine both achievement and performance tasks**. Building self-confidence in your students by providing  opportunities for success and accomplishment is key to promote a joy for learning and to avoid achievement anxiety.

Provide contents that are meaningful to students and, when possible, allow students to define their own learning. You can make tasks more meaningful by connecting content to students' current interest or relating them to their career goals. When possible, give students autonomy to select tasks or topics for learning. Both of these strategies promote students' engagement and offer opportunities to practice social and emotional competencies.

Build regular check-ins with students (both at the beginning and during the day/class). This can take the form of a classroom meeting, but could also be a silent activity where students quickly show you how they are feeling.. You can also use check-in time to ask for feedback about lessons, classroom routines, or particular projects students are developing.

Students bring emotions from life outside of school that influence their disposition to learning. In the classroom, students experience emotions based on the activities, topics, and social interactions that are presented to them. Offering a variety of tasks and activities for students to feel successful, providing engaging content, and allowing for students' autonomy in learning are a few examples of strategies teachers can use to incorporate students' emotions in their planning. And don't forget to have regular check-ins with your students to continue building awareness!

Originally published in Social Emotional Learning and the Common Core blog by Lorea Martinez, Ph.D.

> *Emotions drive us to take action, either by facing the event or by moving away from the situation that produced them.*

2.2 We Feel, Therefore We Learn

By Lorea Martinez, Ph.D.

Emotions drive learning. That is one of the most exciting findings from Immordino-Yang's years of work in affective neuroscience with great implications for teaching and learning. Emotions are an essential piece in the learning process, so how can we foster them in the classroom? What can we do, as educators, to engage students in 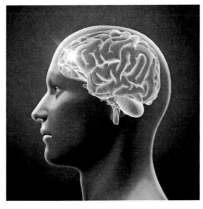 meaningful ways? In my earlier posts, How emotions affect learning part 1 and part 2, I discussed how the emotions students experience in the classroom can affect their disposition to learn. Today, I present 3 key research findings from Immordino- Yang's latest book (one of my summer readings!) Emotions, Learning and the Brain and suggest 3 ways to apply these findings in your classroom.

1. **We only think deeply about things we care about.** According to Immordino-Yang, it is ***neurobiologically impossible*** to build memories, engage complex thoughts or make meaningful decisions without emotion. The brain does not waste energy thinking about things that don't matter to us. This is the reason why learners can pay attention and stay focused when the subjects or topics discussed are *personally relevant* to them.

2. **Emotions guide cognitive learning and decision-making.** Emotions were historically considered

interferences to the learning process, so students were often asked to leave their emotions at the door and just "focus on academic work." Research in affective neuroscience has revealed that emotions are not add-ons, distinct from cognitive skills. Instead, **emotions are the rudder that steers thinking**. Even in academic subjects traditionally considered unemotional, such us physics or engineering, deep understanding depends on making emotional connections between concepts.

3. **Emotional processes help learners apply knowledge in real situations.** Without emotions, students may have certain knowledge, but they likely won't be able to use it effectively when the situation requires. Emotions help learners to recognize and call up relevant knowledge. Emotions are responsible for the application of what students learn in school to novel and real situations.

Are your neurons all fired up by now? There is great potential in using what we now know about the role of emotions in learning to improve teaching and learning. As discussed in an earlier post, being explicit about the social and emotional skills that students need in order to master certain content increases students' effectiveness with the task at hand and builds their self-awareness. Based on Immordino-Yang's work, you can also design educational experiences that encourage **emotional connections with the material being learned**. Here's how.

Give students choices. When students are involved in making decisions about a) their research topic, b) ways to complete a task, or c) showing mastery of a standard, they will likely be more emotionally invested in and attached to the learning outcomes. This is not news for educators, right? Teachers know that choice, when provided in a structured manner, can motivate students and instill a sense of ownership over the learning process.

Help students relate the materials discussed in class to their life and personal interests. Remember that we discussed how the brain doesn't pay attention to things for which we don't care? When students engage with academic material in a meaningful way, they will be able to pay more attention and focus for longer periods of time. An easy way to get to know your students is to have them complete a personal inventory. Discover the topics that are important to them and connect them to the materials discussed in the classroom! These emotional connections will help students apply the content you teach in real life situations. It's a win-win!

Create opportunities to solve open-ended problems. Immordino-Yang argues that highly prescriptive activities are emotionally impoverished. That is to say, they don't allow students to establish the emotional connections that we know are important for cognitive learning and decision-making. Instead, classroom activities should allow students' emotions to appear (comfortable or uncomfortable), along with opportunities for students to make mistakes and learn from them. Project-based learning, group work or even classroom discussions about current events can be effective in letting students wrestle with problems that don't have a right/wrong solution.

Emotions are critical to steering thinking and decision-making. It is neurobiologically impossible to engage complex thoughts or make meaningful choices without emotion. As an educator, you can help students make the emotional connections necessary to drive learning by providing choice, connecting the topics to their lives and interests, and creating opportunities to solve open-ended problems. Give it a try and let me know how it goes!

Originally published in Social Emotional Learning and the Common Core blog by Lorea Martinez, Ph.D.

2.3 Reflecting on the relationship between emotions and learning

Main Ideas. Summarize the main ideas in the articles you just read (How Emotions Affect Learning and We Feel, Therefore We Learn).

Insights. What did you think while reading the text? What did you feel? Were you surprised, worried, excited, etc.?

Direction. What does this mean for your role as a teacher? What are the practical implications for teaching and learning?

2.4 Decoding Emotions

By Joshua Freedman

For most of my life, I found feelings completely confusing. They seemed to happen by themselves, suddenly a feeling would arrive and take over. Now that I've learned more about emotional intelligence, feelings are more making sense to me, but sometimes I still find them confusing.

When you were little, did you ever read the book, *Sometimes I'm Bombaloo?* The girl in that story gets so incredibly angry she feels like she's turned into someone else. I guess everyone sometimes feels overwhelmed by big feelings. Sometimes by anger, but also by sorrow or fear or jealousy or guilt or a big mixed up ball of feelings all rolling together in a thunderstorm. Even excitement can become so big it seems to take over.

People sometimes call emotions like anger and fear "negative" or "bad" feelings, but I've come to see it a different way. Now I believe feelings are just part of us, and they're not good or bad. They're information and energy. What we do with that information and energy could be good or bad. It's like electricity: It's dangerous if you put a fork in the electrical outlet, it can even kill you. But that doesn't mean electricity is bad, it means we need to learn about it and to use it carefully.

Putting Your Toe In

One of the most important steps to learning more about your feelings is to make friends with them. I mean, if you're telling yourself your feelings are confusing and overwhelming and **bad**, then you are not going to be very patient learning about them.

When I was younger, I tried not to think about feelings because they scared me, I felt like they would overwhelm me. I remember in college

I took an acting class, and my teacher, Marie, kept asking me how I was feeling. I was sad and scared because I was far away from the people I loved. One day I told her I didn't like thinking so much about feelings because I thought I might drown in all the feelings. She said, "I'm not asking you to jump into the water, just to put your toe in it."

That was a turning point for me. I experimented with Marie's advice, and I was surprised to learn that I could notice my feelings and tune into them without being overwhelmed by them. I could get closer to my own feelings instead of hiding from them. I could put my toe in the water and it was interesting, not dangerous. I still didn't understand feelings, but they were getting less scary.

Chess Moves

Do you ever play chess? For someone who doesn't know the rules, it's confusing. Why do some pieces go one step, and some jump, and some zoom around in diagonals or lines? If you didn't know any of the rules, it would be hard to play!

I was talking to a work friend named David Caruso about feelings; he said, "Feelings are like chess pieces, there are certain moves they make." This is a surprising idea: there is a logic to feelings. There are basic rules to learn about how they can move and change.

For example, here are three of the rules I've learned:

1. Emotions get more or less intense. Every basic emotion, such as joy or sorrow, fear or trust, can start out small and get bigger. A tiny bit of joy is peace. Add more and it's contentment. Add more to get happiness. More might be pleasure, then delight, then bliss. So imagine someone was feeling peaceful because everything was going well, and then she got even more good news... the feeling would get more intense. Of course, feelings can get less intense too. It's like a color wheel with all these shades and varieties of feelings.

2. Emotions combine. We usually have many feelings at one time. Maybe we're happy to be seeing friends, worried about a test, and sad about an argument... all at the same time! That makes it hard to sort out what we're feeling. Sometimes we name different combinations with a new word. For example, if I'm sad because something didn't go the way I wanted it to, and a little angry that happened, I could call that mixed feeling "disappointed."

3. Emotions focus our attention. We have feelings because something is happening – something inside us or something outside. For example, we have feelings when we think about a choice we've made. If we don't like what we've done there is something going on inside us, so we have a feeling to say "Hey! Notice this, you may have a problem!" That feeling could be called remorse (or guilt or disappointment in ourselves). We have feelings when we see something new and unusual; we could call that surprise or interest. The purpose of an emotion is to get our brains to pay attention to this news.

Emotions as Potions

Imagine you discover this beautiful wooden box carved all over with intriguing symbols. You open the box, and nestled in soft velvet are eight bottles. Each looks different, some are cut crystal sparkly and bright. Some are dark glass with complex swirling designs. Each bottle has a different color potion inside. These potions are the eight basic emotions.

There are around 3000 different words for feelings in English. Where do all those come from? Different researchers have their own theories about what emotions are basic, and what emotions are combinations. There was a scientist named Robert Plutchik who said there are eight basic emotions and they combine in many different ways. Plutchik said we have these emotions because they help us survive.

Here is my interpretation of the way the emotions help us:

Basic Emotion	Why We Have It
Anger	To fight against problems
Anticipation	To look forward and plan
Joy	To remind us what's important
Trust	To connect with people who help
Fear	To protect us from danger
Surprise	To focus us on new situations
Sadness	To connect us with those we love
Disgust	To reject what is unhealthy

You could draw the box with the eight bottles and decide the look and color of each emotion.

What color is Anger? How about Joy? What are their bottles like?

I imagine joy is in very sparkly bright bottle that seems to shine from inside.

The bottles come with a special dropper to release just a little of each one at a time. Imagine you open the bottles and combine drops of these emotions to make incredible potions. The different chemicals mix, changing colors – sometimes the colors stay bright and clear, sometimes they are swirling cloudy and confused. Sometimes sparks come flying out, sometimes a thick fog.

I've never seen a recipe book for this chemistry set, but here are some ideas of how different feelings could be a combination of the basic emotions:

Feeling	Possible Recipe
Impatience	Anger (there is a problem) + Anticipation (looking ahead)
Worry	Fear (danger) + Anticipation (looking ahead)
Boredom	Disgust (rejection) + Sadness (loss) + Fear (risk)
Hope	Anticipation (looking ahead) + Joy (wants fulfilled)

Feeling	Possible Recipe
Respect	Trust (accepting) + Joy (wants fulfilled) + Anticipation (looking ahead)
Disappointment	Sadness (loss) + Anger (there is a problem)
Jealousy	Anger (there is a problem) + Disgust (rejection) + Fear (risk)
Loneliness	Loneliness Sadness (loss) + Fear (risk) + Disgust (rejection)

While this might seem like a fantasy story about wizards, emotions really are chemicals. Like the imaginary box of potions, our brains and bodies produce these different chemicals. The chemicals combine in our bodies and they go into our blood, then they affect every single part of us. Emotions are part of your body's way of communicating with itself.

Reacting to Feelings

One of the most important truths of emotional intelligence comes from learning the difference between feelings, thoughts, and actions.

Imagine your brother messes up your project, you are mad and you tell yourself, "my brother is a jerk" and you hit him.

Notice in that story there is a feeling, a thought, and an action. The three are related, but different. A feeling is just a feeling. The feeling doesn't create the thought or the action. The thought, feeling, and action are influencing each other and they work together to make a problem. On the other hand, you could have the same feeling, the same thought, and a completely different action.

angry   sad   happy

stealthy   bored   excited

What is each guy feeling? What basic emotions are in the recipe for each feeling?

Why do you sometimes use problematic actions? While there are many ways of responding to each situation, most of us tend to use one reaction over and over. In a way, it feels good to get mad and hit. We do that, and we like something about it, and do it again. We KNOW that's not the best solution, but it seems to happen automatically. It's important to remember that behavior is not automatic; it's something we've learned by practicing.

If we've practiced, "when I feel angry, I hit," then we learn that pattern and we tend to use is over and over. Each of us tends to learn several patterns of reacting. For example, do you know someone who tends to "blow up" when they're mad? Or someone who usually gets very quiet when they're upset? Or someone who often leaves the room to get away from an uncomfortable situation?

How about you?

How do you usually react when you're sad? Do you tend to cry, or get mad and blame someone, or pretend not to be sad, or make a joke, or something else?

How do you usually react when you're mad? Do you hit, or say mean words, or get grouchy and prickly, or _____?

A pattern is your usual reaction. When (thought or feeling), I (how you usually react) . For example...

When **I think someone is not listening to me**

I **feel hurt.**

Remember the "observing like a scientist" idea I wrote about in part one? Observe yourself as if you were a scientist studying you. For a few days, notice when you have a big feeling, and notice how you tend to react. Do you fight? Get quiet? Run away? Do you cover your feeling with another feeling? Over time, notice how there are some patterns you use over and over.

When you do find some of your patterns: congratulations! You're making great progress in being smarter about feelings.

> **66**
>
> *Observe yourself as if you were a scientist studying you. For a few days, notice when you have a big feeling, and notice how you tend to react.*
>
> **99**

Don't forget!

1. Emotions are energy and information. They combine, like potions, into many different feelings. They're not good or bad, but each one has a message – a message from one part of you to another part of you.

2. Thoughts, feelings, and actions are not the same.

feeling   thinking   acting

Practice noticing the difference between Feelings, Thoughts, and Actions!

2.5 Getting Off the Trouble Train

By Joshua Freedman

My kids, Emma and Max, have had the same argument about 7 million times. It goes about like this:

1. They're playing and having a great time.

2. Max starts getting a little bored or rebellious so Emma tries to control the game to make it more fun. He feels a bit squished by this, and acts out a little more.

3. Emma doesn't like the way he's messing around, and so she gets fiercer about the rules... and he gets more rebellious.

4. They explode, and eventually end up in time out.

Around step 2, it's obvious (to me and their mom) that they are headed toward the explosion. The momentum builds up, and they both get more and more reactive. The tension builds. Like a train going faster, their fight gets going stronger and stronger. The longer it continues, it becomes harder and harder for them to "get off the train."

I call this kind of situation a Trouble Train — it comes from following patterns that lead to a bigger mess. The "trouble" could be time out or other consequence, or a fight, or even something more serious like stealing or hurting people or breaking something. The "trouble" could also happen inside someone, like a deep sadness or volcano of anger turned against yourself. Some Trouble Trains lead to hurt and sorrow, some lead to conflict, some lead to loneliness. Some Trouble Trains are worse; they could lead to violence, or danger, or jail, or being kicked off a team. While we can learn from these experiences, it would certainly be more pleasant to get off the train before it arrives at these destinations.

Have you ever found yourself in the middle of a situation and you **know** it will to turn into a big mess? You can feel it slipping out of control... and yet you keep going. It's as if you're being pushed along this track; you know it's going to lead to trouble, but it seems like there's no choice.

What's it like for you when that happens? What is the trouble to which it leads you?

Or have you noticed that you often have the same kind of challenges over and over? Maybe you have an argument with your brother or sister or friend... and you can see that same fight happens a lot?

When you're in those situations, you are on the Trouble Train.

You can tell it's a Trouble Train when:

1. You've been on this pathway before – your patterns of reacting are part of the fuel.
2. The situation will result in a consequence that you don't want.

Next Stop: Trouble

Recently Emma and Max were on their usual Trouble Train, and I stopped them and asked: "Do you notice you're on a Trouble Train?" "NO," growled Emma, fiercely trying to get back to her argument. She was so focused on being right and "winning" the argument, she wasn't noticing her reaction.

I can relate to this. When I'm on the Trouble Train, I find it difficult to get off. There seems to be a part of me that WANTS to keep the fight going. For example, sometimes I have an argument with my wife and while I know it's not making life better, I find myself saying just one more point. Or sometimes I feel hurt and I want to hurt her back. I've noticed the longer I am on the train, the harder it is to stop. The energy builds up and up, and my feelings get more and more complicated.

So, an obvious solution is to stop the train fast. When the reaction is just getting started, the situation is not so intense.

Remember in the article "Decoding Emotions" where I wrote about patterns? For example, maybe my pattern is: When I feel hurt, I want to hurt the other person. That one is a "Trouble Train" pattern for me, because when I follow the pattern I definitely get a consequence that I dislike.

When we know our patterns, it's easier to notice and solve the problem BEFORE the train gets going fast.

Sometimes I feel a little hurt, then start getting a little argumentative. The other person says something a bit harsher, and I say something back that's a little mean. They come back with something even meaner, and I want to hit them, but instead I say something really hurtful. Pretty soon we're both hurt and angry, and it's really hard to work out the problem.

In those times, I probably am ignoring my own feelings. I feel a little hurt, but I don't pay attention to that important message, and so I push ahead. Fortunately, I've learned that I have this pattern and I've come to recognize that it's a Trouble Train. So now, sometimes, when I notice myself feeling a little hurt and wanting a little revenge, I can say, "Hey! This is NOT the train I want to take..."

If I notice when I feel just a tiny bit hurt, I can choose a different train. I could solve the problem pretty easily by having a calm conversation, such as:

"When you said _____, I felt hurt. Did you mean to hurt my feelings? Maybe we can take a break and talk about this in a friendly way in a few minutes?"

Remember, just like real trains, Trouble Trains get going faster as you ride them longer. So: The sooner I can notice that I'm on a Trouble Train, the easier it will be to get off!

> *It's easier to solve problems when they are small – when the 'train is going slowly.*

How about you?

Is it hard for you to notice yourself on a Trouble Train?

What feelings "push" you onto a Trouble Train?

What feelings make the train go even faster?

If you could avoid getting on your Trouble Train, how would that help you?

Good news! By carefully noticing your feelings when they're small, you can discover a wonderful secret: **You do not have to get on the Trouble Train.**

However, even if you do get on, there's still hope. You can stop the train before you reach real trouble.

Next Stop: Choice

Ideally, you notice your feelings and patterns before the train even gets going, but sometimes we all get on the train. There's some good news:

You don't have to stay on the Trouble Train!

The first step is to notice you're on that train again. Then, once you notice you're on a Trouble Train, what can you do?

As I said, part of you might want to keep it going, but part of you might want to get off. Just KNOWING that you have a choice is a powerful tool. There's a skill called Exercising Optimism that helps this. If you are feeling helpless and hopeless, you might not believe that you have any choice. In those times, it's useful to remember that many times in the past you have been in difficult situations and found your way through. Also, since nothing lasts forever, this situation will change too. Maybe you can't fix everything, but what is SOMETHING you can do? What is one small step you could take?

It can also be extra complicated in a situation with other people. Maybe you want to stop the train, but they are still pushing it forward. Sometimes when you try to make them stop, the situation seems to get worse, so instead of trying to stop the whole thing, just get yourself off. When you take responsibility for your own choices, that can make it much easier for others to do the same.

One tool for getting off the train is called the Six Second Pause. The purpose is to slow down your reaction and let the emotional energy relax a moment. It works because the chemicals of emotion inside our brains and bodies only last about six seconds. Normally when we have strong feelings, we keep producing more and more of the feeling molecules. But if we can stop for a short moment, the flood of chemicals slows down. The trick with a Six Second Pause is to refocus your brain by shifting attention from the emotional part (the "limbic brain") to the analytical part of your brain (called the "Cortex"). Your Cortex loves to put ideas in order, break ideas apart, and to use symbols like math or language. So, invite your Cortex to the party by doing things it likes, such as:

Solve six math problems.

Remember six words in a foreign language.

Put six favorite songs in alphabetical order.

List six TV characters.

> One of the best ways to step off the Trouble Train is simple: Remember you have choices

Another key to stopping the train is the fact that you have multiple emotions. I wrote about this in the previous chapter. Maybe you feel sad and worried and mad and those feelings are big – they're taking center stage right in the spotlight. At the very same time, maybe you feel caring and committed, but those feelings are hiding in the background. Bring them into the light! Don't let a few of your feelings run the show, invite the others to join.

For example, maybe you are sad about a friend leaving town. Do you have any other feelings? How about happy to have such a good friend? Worried about if you're going to stay close? Excited about when you'll see them again?

Simply recognizing that you have these other feelings can begin to change your emotions. You can intensify the more constructive or useful feelings by naming them, and remembering why you have those feelings. You can intensify any feeling by focusing on it.

Try this! See if you can change your feelings just by focusing on them.

Think of situation where you were annoyed. Remember the annoying details and see if you can feel more annoyed.

Now, think of something funny, and focus on that. See if you can feel more of that silly feeling.

How about sad? Worried? Curious? Happy?

See? You can change your feelings!

Less Fuel

In an old-fashioned steam train, when you shovel more coal into the fire, the train runs faster. What thoughts, feelings, and actions fuel your Trouble Train? You can slow the train by adding opposite thoughts, feelings, and actions.

Here are other techniques for reducing the intensity of the fire:

Heart Breathing: Breathe slowly in counting six full seconds, then breathe out completely over another slow six second count. As you are breathing, focus your attention on your heart, and imagine your heart slowing to a calm beat.

Glow: Imagine yourself filling up with cool, beautiful light. Imagine the light flowing out your fingers.

Warm Layers of Feelings: You might be irritated or hurt or impatient AND underneath that you might have other feelings that are warm and gentle. Notice those gentle feelings and focus on them to make them stronger.

Cotton Candy: Imagine your feelings are like wisps of energy around your body. Imagine scooping up the wisps like they are cotton candy and squeezing them into a yummy treat you can enjoy.

Shrinking: Name your feelings and give them a score from 0 (not present) to 10 (overwhelmingly strong). Imagine these feelings as a ball – imagine the shape, size, and color (e.g., maybe you're angry and scared, it's an 8 in intensity, and you imagine a spiky black and red ball as big as a house). Breathe slowly in and out, and each time you breathe out, imagine your breath cooling the ball causing it to get a little smaller and lighter in color. Imagine this for 30 seconds. Now how intense are the feelings?

Staying Off

One of the best ways to solve the Trouble Train problem is to stay off in the first place! There are always disappointments, differences of opinion, and challenges that could put you on the train, but there are other ways of responding.

If you know your usual Trouble Train (or Trains!!) then it will be easier to avoid them. Maybe you can find a different train that goes someplace more fun?

For example, suppose you have a pattern "When I feel bored, I act annoying to get attention," and this leads you to a Trouble Train. The moment you begin to feel a little bored, consider: Is there another train I could choose to take? Not because someone else is "making me," but because I want to?

Could I connect with someone? Amuse myself? Learn something new? Do some exercise? Read? Draw? Write?

What might happen next?

2.6 Reflecting on decoding and navigating emotions

Main Ideas. Summarize the main ideas in the articles you just read (Decoding Emotions and Getting Off the Trouble Train).

Insights. What did you think while reading the text? What did you feel? Were you surprised, worried, excited, etc.?

Direction. What does this mean for your role as a teacher? What are the practical implications for teaching and learning?

2.7 Assessing Students' EQ

The SEI Youth Version (SEI-YV)

The SEI-YV is intended to help youth grow and thrive. It is suitable for education, counseling, and research.

The report is written to facilitate discussion between adults and youth about the child's current emotional intelligence strengths and challenges. The goal is to help the young person create an action plan to develop effective skills and behaviors at home, at school, and at play.

A classroom or school group report is also available to guide instruction and measure SEL program efficacy.

The SEI-YV includes 74 items assessing the Six Seconds Emotional Intelligence Model, 25 items assessing "Life Barometers," as well as positive impression and mood items.

The SEI-YV norm group is 14,000 and growing, including youth from around the world.

The Youth Version begins with an assessment of five life outcomes called "Barometers of Life" (Good Health, Relationship Quality, Life Satisfaction, Personal Achievement, Self-Efficacy). These provide a context and reason for discussing the youth's EQ.

> *The skills of emotional intelligence are highly correlated with key outcomes, including achievement, good health and positive relationships.*

The EQ scores in the SEI-YV predict **59% of the variation** in these Barometer scores. To increase success in these outcomes, then, a practical approach is to develop the learnable, measurable skills of emotional intelligence following the guidance provided by the SEI-YV.

For more information, go to www.6seconds.org/tools/sei/sei-yv/

Integrating EQ into Classrooms and Schools

Educators agree that it is the responsibility of schools to prepare students to become knowledgeable, responsible, caring adults (Elias et al.,1997). Most educators enter the profession with a belief that education should develop the whole child, including their social and emotional development, but the direction of education in the past few decades has shifted into a focus on test scores and the development of technical skills to the exclusion of the whole person (Darling-Hammond, 2015).

In the 21st century, schools are challenged to serve students who have varying abilities and motivation for learning, and who come from diverse ethnic and socio-economic backgrounds. Attention to the non-cognitive, emotional needs of students has greatly lagged behind in this era of standardized testing and accountability (Darling-

Hammond, 2015). School engagement decreases from elementary to middle to high school, and only half or less of US high school students are engaged in school (Blad, 2014). Engagement is essential for learning and school success.

Moreover, it has been estimated that 30% of high school students participate in high-risk behaviors that affect their school performance and likelihood of life success. Most middle and high school students report that their school did not help them develop social emotional skills like empathy, decision-making, or conflict resolution. A recent study of over 10,000 college students found that they are increasingly anxious and depressed (Hoffman, 2015), and many engage in high-risk behaviors. In addition, a wide college graduation gap exists between affluent students and those of a lower socio-economic status (Dynarski, 2015).

The need for all students to develop Social Emotional Learning (SEL) competencies for college and career readiness and for life success is garnering much needed attention among teachers, school counselors, and administrators. Researchers over the past two decades have successfully demonstrated that SEL skills can be explicitly taught, practiced, modeled, and integrated into student-centered learning, healthy classrooms, and the entire school culture. Successful SEL implementation focuses on universal skills for all students and targeted interventions for students who are facing social, emotional, and/or behavioral challenges. For more information about the importance of EQ and SEL implementation, download Six Seconds' Case for EQ in Schools at http://6sec.org/edcase

3. Social Emotional Learning Implementation

Social and emotional learning (SEL) is the process through which children and adults acquire and effectively apply the knowledge, attitudes, and skills necessary to understand and manage emotions, set and achieve positive goals, feel and show empathy for others, establish and maintain positive relationships, and make responsible decisions. In other words: It's how students learn the skills of emotional intelligence.

Why it Matters

There is overwhelming evidence that our children are facing major social, emotional and mental health obstacles to succeeding at school.

- 21% of teens in the United States reported being bullied on school property. 10.4% of teens reported being hurt by someone they were dating. 17% of students had seriously considered suicide (CDC, 2013 Youth Risk Factors).

- Adding to or exacerbating these problems is the issue of childhood stress, whether from conflict at home, peer pressure, grade pressure, or over-scheduling. Not only can this affect learning in the present, but sustained high levels of cortisol associated with stress can damage the hippocampus, an area of the brain responsible for learning and memory. These cognitive deficits can continue into adulthood (Childhood Stress and Development, CDC, 2008).

- The aim of most SEL programs is to promote self-awareness, self-management, social-awareness, relationships and responsible decision-making skills and to improve students' relationships to their school community and broader world.

> *There is overwhelming evidence that our children are facing major social, emotional and mental health obstacles to succeeding at school.*

SEL/EQ creates an atmosphere where academic performance can thrive, where more positive adult to student and peer to peer relationships flourish, where fewer conduct problems arise, and where lowered stress leads to improved grades and test scores. An effective and well-implemented SEL program can transform a school into a place where children (and the adults who support them) are engaged, curious, safe, and thriving personally and academically.

Six Seconds helps educators create school-wide SEL programs that are integrated, customized and living — so they weave throughout the culture and structure of the school or organization. Schools that teach SEL have lower rates of conflicts, fights, violence, and trips to the principal's office and higher rates of academic success. Six Seconds is committed to research to deepen our understanding and practice of SEL. A recent study of middle school students and school climate is an example of our attention to ground-breaking research. You can read the research here: http://www.6seconds.org/2016/04/14/groundbreaking-education-research-aera/

3.1 Benchmarks for an EQ School Fully Implementing SEL

To effectively implement social emotional learning and teach the essential skills of emotional intelligence, Six Seconds has identified best practices in three key "strands":

- Everyone in the school is developing their own EQ skills
- EQ is integrated into the classrooms to enhance academic learning
- The whole school uses EQ to build a thriving learning community

Three benchmarks comprise each area and a rubric (next page) is provided to assess implementation:

Strand one: **EQ Development**

1. All people in the school community learn & practice EQ.
2. SEL training for educators.
3. Measure EQ to support individual growth.

Strand two: **Extend EQ into the Classroom**

4. EQ data supports teachers for effective practice.
5. EQ extended to support academic learning.
6. EQ used for positive classroom communities

Strand three: **Integrate EQ into the School**

7. Annual SEL planning.

8. EQ visible in school.

9. Use school climate assessment to guide implementation.

Six Seconds has found that, in order to effectively support students and families to practice emotional intelligence, teachers need the training and support to do so themselves. These standards begin by equipping and empowering teachers-as-changemakers to measurably improve education by infusing emotional intelligence into their classrooms and schools. The next stages are to integrate these skills into the classroom and throughout the schools.

Implementation

Stage 1 is usually a pilot group, with implementation across around 25% of the school.

Stage 2 is usually an expansion phase, with implementation to around 50% of the school.

Stage3 is usually an integration phase, with implementation to >90% of the school.

These three "strands" are articulated below at three levels of implementation:

9 Benchmarks	Stage 1	Stage 2	Stage 3
EQ Development 1. Learn & practice EQ 2. SEL training 3. Measure EQ	EQ Lessons for students in selected classes, for at least 8-12 weeks. EQ training and professional development for > 25% of teachers. EQ assessments and informal assessment used in some teacher training or professional development activities and selectively with students.	Consistent EQ activities for >50% stakeholders (students, teachers, parents), at least 20 weeks a year. All SEL (or equivalent) teachers sufficiently trained & certified to facilitate SEL. > 50% Utilize EQ assessments to help guide students, teachers on their development.	Systematic year-long plan (scope/ sequence) of EQ for SEL/Self-Science for all students, teachers, parents Formal SEL training & Certification for >80% of teachers. Students, teachers, parents access EQ assessment in formal planning, goal-setting, learning processes, including staff selection & evaluation.
Extend EQ into the Classroom 4. EQ data 5. EQ supports academic learning 6. EQ classrooms	> 25% teachers supported with individual student EQ data to assist them with challenges. > 25% teachers introduced to ways EQ can be extended to support academic learning. >25% teachers trained in EQ methods for classroom management & community building.	> 50% of teachers use EQ data to help them understand their class and how to best teach them. Evidence of EQ integrated to support academic learning. > 50% teachers actively apply structures & process for building positive classroom community.	Classroom EQ data for coaching/ support of > 80% teachers, leading to a plan for classroom integration. Consistent, daily evidence of EQ supporting academic learning in > 80% classroom. Consistent, daily use of structures & processes for building positive classroom community in >80% classrooms.
Integrate EQ into the School 7. SEL planning 8. EQ everywhere 9. School climate assessment	Process for setting annual goals for SEL. Leaders advocate for importance of SEL as a foundation for school's success. Formal or informal methods for assessing school climate and SEL implementation at least on annual basis.	Annual leadership meeting focused on SEL plan & with specific commitments. Make SEL visible throughout the school including policies, procedures, plant. Informal assessments plus annual use of school climate and other assessments to track SEL implementation.	Strategic plan with specific goals, designated leaders & plans for SEL to include annual review and report. Mission includes SEL as a central pillar, visible throughout the school including policies, procedures & plant. Systematic use of formal and informal assessment to guide SEL implementation.

Examples of Implementing the Benchmarks

To assist educators in envisioning ways these benchmarks can be implemented, here is a selection of possible strategies.

EQ Development

1. All people learn & practice EQ

- Ongoing coaching or peer coaching for faculty and staff.

- Regularly scheduled EQ workshops for teachers to understand themselves and each other and practice their own EQ skills for personal development.

- Experienced, emotionally intelligent adults participating & facilitating weekly Self-Science/SEL classes – where adults are modeling and honestly engaging.

- Training on EQ skills, norms, and expectations specifically for partners, volunteers, subcontractors, bus drivers, maintenance staff, security personnel, and other adults who are part of the school community.

- Regularly scheduled "Parent EQ camp" events with a series of workshops/lessons over time.

- Monthly EQ newsletter for parents & teachers highlighting a key concept or monthly theme for EQ focus.

2. SEL training for educators

- Monthly 2-hour "EQ Lab" sessions led by SEL team with free and easily accessible resources.

- An EQ Educator Certification for all teachers, counselors, and school leaders to develop own EQ and learn how to integrate it into their practice, using the Self-Science curriculum.

- Certification in Six Seconds' EQ Assessments for adults and youth, individuals and groups.

- A series of Six Seconds' CORE courses for a deeper dive into EQ for personal transformation and meaningful professional development.

3. Measure EQ to support individual growth

- The Six Seconds Youth Version assessment (SEI-YV) and/ or Perspective on Youth for Teacher or Parents (pYV) used annually for students in goal setting and guiding instruction.

- SEI (Adult Version) used annually for all staff for their goal setting & professional development.

- SEI Profiles used in parent workshops.

Extend EQ into the Classroom

4. EQ data supports teachers.

- Students take the SEI-YV for full SEI-YV report or the shorter Brain Profiles reports for teacher, counselor, administrator use.

- Classroom "Dashboard" reports and a 1-1 coaching session for each teacher looking at their EQ skills in relation to their classroom; follow-up coaching sessions to support them to make and follow plans to best support their classroom's EQ.

- A Team Vital Signs Assessment (TVS) for teaching team / level team to understand how they can best work together.

5. EQ extended to support academic learning.

- Classroom observations and coaching focused on use of EQ skills, vocabulary, processes in academic lessons.

- Informal mechanisms for evaluating group process such as a reflection question to the class after group work is completed about "what went well, what could be better next time?"

- Group work assignments specifically state which EQ skills are being used / developed / assessed.

- Use of "Fusion Questions" in class discussion (blending cognitive and emotional thinking, such as, "If you where the character in the book, what decision would you make, and how would that feel?"

- Six Seconds' Learning Philosophy principles are instrumental in lesson planning.

- Lessons use Six Seconds' lesson template, incorporating Engage/Activate/Reflect (EAR) framework.

- Deliberate use of current neuroscience findings, e.g. mini-breaks for active movement.

- SEL lessons use Six Seconds' lesson format template, highlighting EQ Competencies/Talents and Link to Academic Standards (e.g. Common Core).

6. EQ used for positive classroom communities

- Regular "check-ins" about emotions, especially after transitions (e.g. after lunch).

- Class meeting/circle time used for building safety, listening, group development.

- Growth Mindset informs culture.

- Mindfulness practices.

- Social problem-solving.

- EQ process used for decision-making.

- EQ basis for classroom management / behavior management.

- Restorative justice practices.

- Support of and honoring of diversity, inclusion, embracing of differences and respect for people of all orientations and backgrounds so all people feel welcome for who they are.

Integrate EQ into the School

7. Annual SEL planning

- SEL Professional Learning Community including teachers, parents, administrators, and even students, meeting regularly to review and plan in advance to promote adult and student competencies and success.

- Director of SEL (or equivalent) empowered and supported to lead EQ implementation in partnership with school administration.

- Ongoing, regular meeting to review EQ progress, including participation from senior leadership.

- Specific budget/funding for EQ / SEL.

- Board committee and/or Parent Association committee dedicated to supporting administration in building and maintaining positive climate.

8. EQ visible in school.

- Development and annual review of policies to support an "EQ community" including Communication Policy, Conflict Resolution / Problem-Solving Policy, Decision-making process/ criteria.

- Intentionally bring EQ into every meeting by starting with a check-in or brief EQ exercise.

- Teachers-as-SEL-researchers finding and sharing best practices through writing, speaking, blog posts, education events.

- Annual EQ retreat for board to experience their own EQ development, review current data, and collaborate on how they can best support the school climate.

- Evidence of EQ visible throughout the school facilities through posters, signs, materials created by students & teachers to reinforce the skills and vocabulary.

- Wellness initiatives to support teacher self-care, such as special breakfasts, meditation groups, exercise activities, and Self-Science classes for teachers to feel connected and supported as people.

- Job descriptions state the importance of emotional intelligence.

9. Use school climate assessment to guide implementation.

- Regularly measure school climate and use this data as a focus for ongoing growth, meetings with administration, faculty, parents, and students to review & plan – then re-measure. After each assessment, the administration meets to review the results with a facilitator, and then meets with all faculty/staff to review the results and set goals. The administration and faculty hold a meeting with parents, and optionally others with students.

- Aggregate student & adult EQ data into an annual synthesis to help prioritize when making the SEL plans.

For citations: Freedman, J., Jensen, A. L., Stillman, S. B., & McCown, K. (2016). Benchmarks for an EQ school fully implementing SEL.

For an example of a school fully implementing SEL:

Stillman, S. B., Stillman, P., Martinez, L., Freedman, J., Jensen, A. L., & Leet, C. (2017). Strengthening social emotional learning with student, teacher, and schoolwide assessments. *Journal of Applied Developmental Psychology*. https://doi.org/10.1016/j.appdev.2017.07.010

3.2 Using the Benchmarks at Your School

Based on your reading of the benchmarks for an EQ school fully implementing SEL, what is one area you are committed to strengthen? Write where you are now in the first section, Now. What would you like to accomplish in 90 days? Write that in the last third section, 90 Days. In the middle, write an action plan outlining the specific actions you can take now and those you'd take later to meet your goal. Feel free to use another sheet of paper.

3.3 Teaching in the Age of Selfies

By Anabel Jensen, Ph.D.

Welcome to the Age of Selfies, where we are so self-absorbed, self-promotional, and self-conscious we've lost connection with others. Is there anything we do to counteract it? Using emotional intelligence will help increase compassion and empathy. EQ in the classroom or boardroom helps build bridges between people and gets us to break free from the Age of Selfies. Here's 6 how-to tips to build stronger relationships and help use emotional intelligence to increase compassion and empathy.

Reject Rejection

Think back for a moment to your first day at school when you were fix or six. Or, remember the first day of middle or high school. Were you feeling anxious, scared, or worried about being rejected? For most people, this was a day of nervous excitement—an opportunity to discover new friends, and to explore an environment in which you would be spending the next few years. Perhaps you were shy or timid—sure you would spend the next years alone—unable to make new friends, or worried that you might look or seem different from the others.

Would you be rejected because of your brilliant red hair or your Italian nose? Even now—as old as I am—I identify and relate with these new and worrisome moments from visiting new countries or participating in that vegan cooking class— that these stresses are very real and distracting in the first few seconds of a new *experience*, but for young people, beginning at a new school, or switching classes, is an especially stressful and emotionally challenging time.

So, I began to think about how teachers can help during these tricky moments when students might feel isolated, or worried that they won't fit in. Straight away, I wondered if the strands of thought and behavior which we're increasingly seeing in modern society – selfishness, egotism, the dismissing of others who are too different from ourselves – might be impacting today's students' social and educational experiences in the classroom. Perhaps the best question is: how could they not? Movies, pop music, TV shows, and above all social media have all become conduits, it appears to me, for a new level of suspicion and disdain; our discourse has, partly due to the very mediums we use, become troublingly curt, brief, and often ego-driven. It appears our society is becoming more and more narcissistic and less and less empathetic. Here's 6 how-to rules on how I try to teach tolerance and acceptance using emotional intelligence in the classroom.

Rule 1: Empathy Above All Else

I have always had the aim of helping students to become both academically and *personally* successful. The building of key skills such as compassion and altruism takes time and focus, but in the context of this troubling, xenophobic tone we're hearing from society in many corners, I feel it's never been more important to take the time, effort, and energy to teach the necessary emotional and social skills. A student's classmates will be vitally important for learning to perceive and then practicing empathy, but the momentum and direction must invariably be modeled by the teacher.

Rule 2: Laugh About It

Classrooms can be stuffy places where students feel intimidated and inhibited. To break down some of these barriers, I'm always ready to laugh at myself, and to find ways of bringing a smile to my students' faces. I bring in jokes that connect with the subject matter and encourage students to do the same. If we're laughing, the task of learning doesn't seem so challenging, and the awkwardness of being singled out, for example, in front of one's classmates, is mitigated. Mistakes become less important and more trivial, and not occasions for worry or self-doubt.

> *Openness, love and a readiness to communicate will assist my students in making friends and taking a realistic, evidence-based view of the world.*

Rule 3: Listening is Learning

This is a very subtle task. We often think we are listening, but often we are planning our next words or a clever rebuttal. So, for my students I always emphasize listening to each other and respecting the comments that classmates make. This can be done very simply, through simple gestures ('wait', 'carry on', 'say that again', 'say more about that') and facial expressions which connote my enthusiasm for the lives of others, and my good-natured concern that some classmates might not be listening as attentively as I'd prefer.

Rule 4: Walking in Another's Shoes

Readings, role-plays and class discussions are good opportunities to tease out those moments in life where optimism or consequential thinking might usefully come into play. If you're reading about the European migrant crisis, for instance, you might ask your students to verbalize just what a migrant has been through, and to imagine their fear and insecurity. What EQ skills might benefit these individuals? When examining government policies, hone in on the individual people who might be impacted, and imagine the effect of the policy on their day-to-day lives. What EQ skills might be needed here? All of these questions emphasize the practice of *humanizing* others; when doing this, we tend to find that their troubles and desires are *just as legitimate as our own.* Finding a solution together for a tussle on the playground (empathy) might be as simple as imagining the world from someone else's point of view; successfully debating and negotiating the stops in a class field trip often comes from standing in their classmates' shoes. We can never do enough of this.

Rule 5: In Praise of Empathy

We can make empathy a habit. Habit guru Charles Duhigg says, "If you can identify the right cue and reward—you can establish almost any habit." When students seize upon an opportunity for empathy, make a point of thanking them for doing so. When you see them practicing their optimism when a big test is approaching, congratulate them. When you notice they are identifying the pros and cons of a decision, celebrate. Each example adds to your students' store of knowledge and experience, and very gradually builds up a tendency to seek out ways to think differently about how they treat others and the decisions they will make. Of course, doing so is its own reward, but a word of gratitude reinforces just how positive this manner of thinking can be.

Rule 6: Class Credo Over Rules

I have found through 77 years of experience, that every meeting, table talk, seminar, workshop, and/or even graduate classes needs a short page of 'rules' by which all agree to abide. Creating these together—along with the consequences of breaking the rules—makes it easier to enforce them. In fact, the individuals/students will point out when a rule is being broken. So, I've found initialing a formal-looking contract to be an excellent method of focusing my students' (from kindergarteners to graduate students) minds on their attitudes and behavior. I keep a copy of the agreement pinned to the classroom wall for ready reference during those moments where a student forgets. The list should include encouragements to listen to each other, respect a variety of opinions, and never to make disparaging remarks about someone's appearance or background. In this sense, it becomes a class *Credo*, defining and articulating the group's guiding principles. Also, on the list should be: treat everyone fairly. Here, I use Thomas Jefferson's definition of equality:

By its very nature, a deliberate policy of giving everyone what they need in terms of time and attention shows your students: **1) that they are all valued,** and **2) that the amount of the teacher's time a student receives is defined neither by their gender or ethnic group, nor by their level of academic achievement.**

One way I check up on myself as whether I am meeting my goal is to record my class (audio or video, preferably both). I always discover some unexpected traits or habit of which I was not aware. A sober and responsible review of these recordings can – in my experience – teach me as much about changes I need to make as a formal visit from the principal or superintendent.

Being Open to Life Lessons

Both teachers and their students will always be living in an arena of uncertainty—filled with expected challenges often followed by hopelessness and helplessness. I believe it is my responsibility to provide a more humanistic way of seeing the world. I like to contrast isolationism with inclusion and acceptance, and to demonstrate that hatred and suspicion are very *infrequently* justified.

What are you doing in your meetings or classroom to build and reinforce emotional intelligent behavior? Openness, love and a readiness to communicate will assist my students in making friends and taking a realistic, evidence-based view of the world. The teacher who creates the circumstances in which students develop these emotional intelligence skills is the teacher whom the students remember forever and strive to emulate.

Originally published in Emotional Intelligence: Yoga for the Mind by Anabel Jensen, Ph.D.

3.4 Back to School with Hope, Optimism, and Maybe, Something More?

By Joshua Freedman

I always loved+dreaded this back-to-school time of year. Dreaded because it meant the end of lazy afternoons stretching from freedom to boredom. But more, loved, because as a child (later as a teacher), a new school year meant a clean slate – infinite possibility – even redemption: Maybe this year will be better?

Back to School with a Clean Slate

I love that expression: "A clean slate." I guess back in the day, slates got choked with the dust of diligent work. In my childhood, the "dust" was an accumulation of disappointments grinding away at my sunny disposition. Maybe, I'd think each new school year, maybe year would be **new**. So new that it would make me anew.

School-year after school-year, I remember days of throwing my paper-bag lunch into my backpack, and over and over, by mid-day the yogurt would break open and soak into my textbooks. *Maybe would be the year they stopped breaking?*

From as-early-as-I-can-remember until my third year of college, I was always behind on work. I loathed the late-Sunday realization that I wasn't prepared for Monday. *Maybe would be the year I stayed on top of my homework?*

I always felt like an outsider looking in. I had friends, but I was also lonely. Playing games like four-square at lunch, I'd be welcome to join, but rarely invited. *Maybe this would be the year the cool kids would ask me to play?*

These stories are simplifications of a deeper fear. The hope for renewal, for change, was tied to all of my (our?) worst fears: Will I fit in? Will I find my way through this maze? Will I be loved? Will I sit alone at lunch?

I wonder now, if my teachers had any idea how I felt, if they could glimpse my hopeless hope. I wonder if teachers reading this now might see more deeply into their new students. Could they gently understand the desperate longing that will soon fill the seats of their classrooms?

Teachers: How do you imagine your students are feeling that first day of school? **What do you want them to feel** in the first minutes... first hours... by the end of the day? Recognizing there might be a vast gap between how they feel walking in and how you want them to feel, what can you do to close the gap?

Optimism is Hope with a Plan

These examples sound sad to me, but I wasn't sad, I was abundantly (overly?) hopeful. I was a cheerful puppy bounding through the obstacles, not letting them get me down, but not changing. Is that optimism?

In the Six Seconds Model, we describe the emotional intelligence competency as: Exercise Optimism. Wishes are beautiful, gossamer creations of dream and longing. Optimism has sweat on its brow. I didn't have a plan, I didn't take the ownership of the solution. Yet unbeknownst to me, time was working within me, and something unfolded.

I had a wish, "somehow it would be different," but no real intention to change. Now decades later, I'd like to go back and hug myself; gently, firmly I'd say: **You have choices, and your choices will make your future.** And while that's absolutely true, I'm a bit surprised to realize: Determination is only part of the story.

The Power of Long Summer Afternoons

I could hardly wait to start school to see if the long summer afternoons had transformed something in me, in us. I had this sense of discovery, of boldly going someplace new — and *possibly* wonderful.

On one hand, it was nonsense, and each year led to inevitable disappointments and dashed hopes. My hastily thrown-together lunch inevitably spilled. My near-total lack of interest in the meaningless homework continued to mean a growing collection of late slips. My earnest lack of attention to social skills meant I remained a dork.

But at the very same time I was right, year after year.

Somehow, eventually, I learned to leave my yogurt in my locker instead of my lunchbox. Somehow I found academic work (and writing) that I loved, and even became a straight-A student. Miraculously I met wonderful people who love me for who I am. It reminds me of one of the most beautiful quotes of all time, from Rabindranath Tagore, winner of the 1913 Nobel Prize in Literature:

> *Not hammer-strokes, but dance of the water, sings the pebbles into perfection.*

There is, it seems, a magic in those slowly passing summer days. They are a dance of water. They are our parents telling us a million times to be better. They are the careful practice. They are the power of trying again, and again, and again. And something more.

We often use phases such as, "drive change" or "change management" or "lead change" — but maybe change leads us? Maybe change isn't something that is "driven" by force and control... maybe change is, in its deepest way, a process of unfolding.

Of course, passing days isn't enough. Time doesn't teach us all we need to know. For me, the catalyst was finding a place where I fit. Of learning something about work that matters, something about participating in the world.

In my child-mind it would all happen by itself with the dawning of a new year. Later I thought I could simply make it be. Now, I glimpse that change is not linear correlation between work and commitment. There's no "breakthrough," no one point where step one becomes step two. The journey of growth is woven with chaos... and not done yet. Persistent work is required, but it's not enough. For me, luck was a big help, but again, not enough. The real "dance of water" comes from all these, plus belonging, love, and, so powerfully the realization grows: **My choices matter.**

> 66
>
> *Wishes are beautiful, gossamer creations of dream and longing. Optimism has sweat on its brow.*
>
> 99

The Catalyst of Purpose

Yes, of course my choices determine if the yogurt explodes all over my backpack, but it's more than that. Of course, my choices determine if my homework is on time, but that doesn't touch on the deeper Why. Finding friends, and love, is closer.

The real catalyst, the lever for change, grew slowly as I grew deeper connections with the world around me. The summer afternoons turned into a gradual understanding: I have a part to play. It's one small part in a big cast, but I'm the only one who can fill this role, the world needs me to be me. Even more, as understanding of interconnectedness grows, my purpose becomes more clear. Finally, I begin to see a new glimmer: My choices matter because my choices become the dance of water for others.

Now here we are again, back near the start of another year of school. The long summer afternoons are fading, and it's time to go back to class. Yet maybe it will be different? Here we are in these days of raw potential — of renewal, of hope, of infinite possibility. Even long past days when September marked new books and school clothes, the echoes of this potential stayed with me. That feeling of please-don't-let- summer-end blends with wonder and gratitude for what we can become.

3.5 Assessing your school's SEL implementation

In this chapter, we have described the SEL implementation process for an EQ school. The process is described using three key strands with three benchmarks each. Use the following rubric to identify where your school activities fit into broader schoolwide SEL implementation, so you can help your school take SEL to the next level. For each benchmark, circle the description in stage 1, 2 or 3 that best describes your school.

Strand one: EQ Development

	Stage 1	Stage 2	Stage 3	What could you/your school do to go to the next level?
1. All people in the school community learn & practice EQ	EQ Lessons for students in selected classes, for at least 8-12 weeks.	Consistent EQ activities for >50% stakeholders (students, teachers, parents), at least 20 weeks a year.	Systematic year-long plan (scope/sequence) of EQ for SEL/Self-Science for all students, teachers, parents	
2. SEL training for educators	EQ training and professional development for > 25% of teachers.	All SEL (or equivalent) teachers sufficiently trained & certified to facilitate SEL.	Formal SEL training & Certification for >80% of teachers	
3. Measure EQ to support individual growth	EQ assessments and informal assessment used in some teacher training or professional development activities and selectively with students.	> 50% Utilize EQ assessments to help guide students, teachers on their development.	Students, teachers, parents access EQ assessment in formal planning, goal-setting, learning processes, including staff selection & evaluation	

Circle the description in stage 1, 2 or 3 that best describes your school. Write what action items you and/or your school would need to take to advance to the next level.

Strand two: Extend EQ into the Classroom

	Stage 1	Stage 2	Stage 3	What could you/your school do to go to the next level?
4. EQ data supports teachers for effective practice	> 25% teachers supported with individual student EQ data to assist them with challenges.	> 50% of teachers use EQ data to help them understand their class and how to best teach them.	Classroom EQ data for coaching/ support of > 80% teachers, leading to a plan for classroom integration	
5. EQ extended to support academic learning	> 25% teachers introduced to ways EQ can be extended to support academic learning.	Evidence of EQ integrated to support academic learning.	Consistent, daily evidence of EQ supporting academic learning in > 80% classroom.	
6. EQ used for positive classroom communities	>25% teachers trained in EQ methods for classroom management & community building.	> 50% teachers actively apply structures & process for building positive classroom community.	Consistent, daily use of structures & processes for building positive classroom community in >80% classrooms.	

Circle the description in stage 1, 2 or 3 that best describes your school. Write what action items you and/or your school would need to take to advance to the next level.

Strand three: Integrate EQ into the School

	Stage 1	Stage 2	Stage 3	What could you/your school do to go to the next level?
7. Annual SEL planning	Process for setting annual goals for SEL.	Annual leadership meeting focused on SEL plan & with specific commitments	Strategic plan with specific goals, designated leaders & plans for SEL to include annual review and report.	
8. EQ visible in school	Leaders advocate for importance of SEL as a foundation for school's success.	Make SEL visible throughout the school including policies, procedures, plant.	Mission includes SEL as a central pillar, visible throughout the school including policies, procedures & plant.	
9. Use school climate assessment to guide implementation	Formal or informal methods for assessing school climate and SEL implementation at least on annual basis.	Informal assessments plus annual use of school climate and other assessments to track SEL implementation.	Systematic use of formal and informal assessment to guide SEL implementation.	

4. Six Seconds Learning Philosophy

The Six Seconds' Learning Philosophy comprises the core beliefs about learning that shape our approach to teaching, learning, and practicing EQ. We are actively committed to these principles; therefore, they inform how we design and deliver trainings, create products, and structure programs. We expect these principles to be seen, felt, and experienced in every product, lesson, or event, including this book! We invite you to try on these principles in the hope that they will become yours as well. Each of the six principles is explained below, with a paragraph on Meaning, Interpretation, and Putting it into Action.

Here are some questions to think about as you read the Learning Philosophy principles:

- What does this principle mean to you?

- How would your teaching change if you adopted one or more of these Learning Philosophy principles?

- How would that change the experience for your students?

What key principles will guide effective practice for learning?

4.1 *Six Principles of Learning*

Wisdom Lives Within

Meaning: Learners have deep expertise inside them already, so a key aim of learning is to draw that out.

Interpretation: People learn best when they construct meaning vs. if we "tell them the secret." This principle is about blossoming and unfolding; growing and transforming. Our job is to create an environment/experience where people can find their own answers. Self-reflection is key!

In action: Ask, don't tell. Provide time and space for reflection. Share your own insights. Validate answers — focus on the deeper concepts vs. "right answers". Don't read slides — ask good questions about slides.

No Way is The Way

Meaning: Learners each integrate and apply knowledge in unique ways, so flexibility and personalization is essential to effective learning.

Interpretation: There is no such thing as "1 size fits all," so we need to differentiate and personalize. We need flexibility and space for people to develop authentic, powerful, individual solutions. People learn in a variety of ways, and we need to teach to many learning styles. We also need to adapt and flex to effectively work with the complexities of real people.

In action: Engage many different learning styles so different people can learn in their own best ways. In each conclusion, participants are encouraged to do their own synthesis and craft their own authentic next steps.

The Process is the Content

Meaning: The experience of learning shapes the meaning of the learning.

Interpretation: Optimal learning comes from role modeling; talk the talk + walk the walk. Create a powerful learning process of Engage, Activate, Reflect[1]. Learning comes from experiencing and reflecting — doing, thinking, and feeling. Our job is to model and to use our own emotional intelligence so others can develop theirs.

In action: Use an experiential approach with many opportunities for discovery — as well as powerful conceptual theories. Facilitators will be most successful if they model their own emotional intelligence in setting up and debriefing the process.

1,2,3 PASTA!

Meaning: To be useful, learning must be applied and put into action.

Interpretation: Powerful learning comes to life through action; it's not only an internal process. If people don't take action with what they've learned, we have not changed their

---

[1] For more tips about using the Engage-Activate-Reflect process, read section 4.2 and 5.

lives and improved the world. So we need to help them put new ideas into action.

In action: Foster the feelings of anticipation, excitement, joy to motivate action. Invite participants to identify how to put ideas into action and next steps. Be sure to save time for this important component.

Fish Don't Talk About Water

Meaning: Learning something new requires a new perspective or dissonance.

Interpretation: While distress undermines learning, some stress is valuable; this means learners and facilitators need to move out of the comfort zone into the stretch zone. It takes a moderate level of dissonance to learn and to gain new perspectives. Our job is to make it safe enough for people to go beyond comfort and conformity and to gently push them toward the land of the unknown. Your affect will influence this greatly —  if you quickly establish trust in the group, the exercise will give them a new and valuable perspective on themselves and their work.

In action: Do activities and hold discussions that create a small degree of discomfort, encouraging participants to look at situations in new ways. Talk about the "elephant in the room" in a respectful open way.

Emotions Drive People

Meaning: Emotions are central to effective learning.

Interpretation: We don't create meaning with emotion or analysis alone; optimal learning integrates feeling + thinking and action! Create learning experiences that involve Head + Heart + Hands. Emotions are valuable signals that help us survive and thrive. When we learn how to use them, emotions help us make more effective decisions, connect with others, find and follow purpose — and lead a more whole-hearted life.

In action: Connect to your own emotions and those of others. Consider emotional consequences in decision making and performance. Share your own emotions involved in a situation and in decision making with others, and elicit their emotional connection to the learning and change process.

How can you apply the Learning Philosophy in your teaching?

In the spaces next to each Learning Philosophy principle below, write how you might practice each one in your teaching or in your personal life.

Wisdom Lives Within

No Way is the Way

The Process is the Content

1-2-3 Pasta

Fish Don't Talk About Water

Emotions Drive People

4.2 Hallmarks of a Great EQ-Powered Lesson

Use this checklist to evaluate your lessons.

How many of these best practices are you incorporating?

Be "smart with feelings" in your learning design. Many of these methods engage "hot cognition,"

a highly activated brain state where optimal learning can occur. By using practices like these, educators can improve retention and strengthen students' ability to process information – and make school into a more positive experience for everyone involved.

Engage: Create a powerful hook	
	Draw students in, tell a story, ask a powerful question, show a video, read a poem
	Set an interesting, worthwhile goal; link to students' current passion/interests
	Share intriguing data or a substantive model/graphic organizer to frame learning
	Stir in emotion [Emotions Drive People]
Activate: Multiply learning through senses & fun	
	Add interesting, even beautiful, visuals or other media
	Create dissonance, surprise or wonder through something provocative, funny, unusual, or a powerful personal story [Fish Don't Talk About Water]

	Divide class period into chunks of <20 min each including opportunities to play with ideas, to make a game with content [The Process is the Content]
	Let students take ownership of "how" and adapt the learning to their interests & how they learn best [No Way is The Way]
Reflect: Invite students to make meaning & commit to action	
	Ask powerful questions and invite students to share responses with partners or group or journal [Wisdom Lives Within]
	Challenge students to come up with one action they can take to bring the learning out of the classroom and into their lives [1,2,3 Pasta]

Adapted from Hot Cognition Checklist by Anabel Jensen and Joshua Freedman of www.6seconds.org for Facebook's InspirED

> 66
>
> *Use your emotional intelligence to design learning that is highly engaging and fuels positive growth.*
>
> 99

4.3 *Neuroscience in Learning*
Learning About Learning & the Brain
by Joshua Freedman

At a neurological level, how does the brain actually learn, and what's the role of emotion? What's the implication for education and training? From around the globe, members of the Six Seconds community identified key questions they wanted Joshua Freedman to discuss with Dr. Mary-Helen Immordino-Yang about four key themes:

1. Activating the brain for learning.

2. Engaging curiosity.

3. Creating the optimal state for learning.

4. Maintaining a focus on long-term vision.

Much has been discussed about creating "ideal learning environments" in classrooms around the world. But what about inside the student's mind? In a recent NYT article Mary-Helen Immordino-Yang discusses the biological conditions for learning. She states "it is literally neurobiologically impossible to think deeply about things that you don't care about." In conversation with Josh Freedman, she discusses these findings.

Josh: Mary Helen, you had a New York Times interview recently, and in the article, it said, "It is literally neurobiologically impossible to think deeply about things that you don't care about." So, what's the implication for educators?

Mary Helen: I think it has huge implications. Let's back up: That feature of our biology makes perfect evolutionary sense. Why would you waste time spending energy and effort and neurological resources on thinking about random things that don't have any bearing on anything important? That would be a silly use of energy.

This has important implications for the way in which we design assessment, for example. I think a lot of the reason why we have these assessment systems set up on the way they do with all kinds of implications for what happens to you next. These big tests are mainly designed to deal with this attention problem. If the tests weren't there, there'd be no intrinsic reason why the person would bother caring to think about this, right?

Josh: So, in other words, if we say to kids, "The reason you should care about this is because it's on the test."

Mary Helen: Exactly.

Josh: But aren't tests motivating because they are important?

Mary Helen: Well, no. We're activating the brain for learning, but in a very superficial, shallow way. The emotion has to be there to be able to think about stuff. So, if there's no intrinsic interest in the material, no reason that that kid subjectively ought to engage in the information, we resort to things like, "Well, it's going to be on the test." As a way to sort of slap emotion on from the outside. Saying, "Well, there's no reason why this is interesting, so we've got to make it important somehow. So, we're going to give you some external standard by which to measure success."

Josh: [Laughs] So in a way, we're telling learners: "be scared."

Mary Helen: Yeah. Exactly. Be scared and do something about it because I have no other way to motivate you, basically. It's a cop-out on the part of the education system.

Josh: But, isn't fear motivating?

Mary Helen: Well, sure. But, here's the thing. A small amount of it is, but, we rely on it far, far too heavily. I mean, fear is motivating, but fear, like any emotion, has a characteristic, cognitive pattern that is a piece of the emotion itself.

When you feel afraid it shifts your thought patterns and your memory. Fear means keeping yourself safe or to fight, right? And so, you are shaping the very nature of the knowledge construction of the skill construction in any academic domain to be sort of organized around fight and flight and escape strategies.

And those are not conducive to deep engagement with the ideas and their intrinsic interests. Their fear and curiosity are completely opposites in terms of the way in which they engage condition and memory. When you're curious you're open, you're safe, you're in a kind of intellectually playful place in which you're sort of exploring possibilities.

When you're afraid you narrow yourself to a very efficient, focused escape strategy, like, "Get me out of here, quick. I just memorize this, and I'm done? Okay. I'll do that." So, you're directly undermining the development of interest and curiosity and long-term learning when you do that.

Josh: So if a goal of learning is meaning making, we've got to find more effective emotional "hooks" to engage curiosity.

Mary Helen: Right.

> ❝
>
> *Many of our educational practices in traditional educational environments directly undermine a person's development of a proclivity toward a curious mind state.*
>
> ❞

Engaging curiosity

Curiosity is an aroused state of the brain that has complex and interconnected processes at play. Mary-Helen Immordino-Yang discusses the neurological state of curiosity for learning. Her groundbreaking research on curiosity will inform educators everywhere.

Josh: What's the neurological role of curiosity?

Mary Helen: What's happening when we're curious? We know something about this and not enough about this. When you're curious you are engaging in a kind of exploration of an idea, and that exploration is leading you. It's motivating you and it's leading you to engage with and follow things that you notice. So, think about the inherent subjectivity and skillfulness in that process. You have to know what's worth noticing and what isn't worth noticing. And so, you're developing a sort of intellectual intuition.

That is an inherently a nuanced, implicit and emotional process. "I am recognizing that that is important, and potentially useful. But, I don't actually fully understand it." Think about all the metacognitive processes that go into those three calculations. These assessments are experientially-based and also connected to motivation and engagement.

Many of our educational practices in traditional educational environments directly undermine a person's development of a

> *As society changes, education has to move with it and be a supportive force towards a new kind of world.*

proclivity toward a curious mind state. A curious state is one in which you explore and notice, and follow what you've noticed... and try to play it out... and question yourself about whether or not you fully understand and appreciate it... Then, come back around where you were before and re-examine what you thought you already knew, potentially with a new understanding of something else that might be related or a new connection.

Too much focus on external evaluation or product may reduce curiosity. But there are good pedagogical strategies that are known to increase curiosity and the kind of thought process that are known to support it. An example is really well-designed project-based learning.

That said, sometimes a kid isn't currently interested in a topic because they don't have enough knowledge or experience in that space to develop the sense of curiosity. In these cases, it is the job of the educational experience is to expose them to the relevance of it. Teach them so it feels important, then they can develop and foster a sense of curiosity in that domain.

Creating the optimal state for learning

Educators wanting to refine their practice may be thinking they can create an optimal environment for brain-based learning. Dr. Immordino-Yang helps us refocus by looking at the goals of learning we are trying to purse. What kind of learning, skill and practices do we want students to be capable of doing? This will inform the kind of teaching and environment we should create.

Josh: I was just in China teaching, and one of the things that was super challenging was that, in Six Seconds' methodology, we focus on the teacher not being the one with the answers. But in the Chinese cultural context, that was seen as, "bad teaching."

Mary Helen: The teacher not having the answers?

Josh: Right. There must've been something wrong with me because I didn't have the answers. Even though I told the students, "In this class I'm not going to give you the answers," it was very uncomfortable for them. And, of course, that discomfort has some benefits and some costs from a learning perspective. So, I'm wondering: how much do you need to kind of go with the cultural norms, even if in some ways those cultural norms are not aligned with how the brain learns best?

Mary Helen: That's a really good question. That's a really deep question. So, I'm going to kind of challenge a couple of the assumptions that are listed in that question, okay?

Josh: Okay.

Mary Helen: The first thing I would say is that, this style of learning where the teacher has the answers and the kids were meant to try to discover them is not how the brain learns best. That's a particular kind of learning. It's the most efficient way to get to a certain kind of learning. What we need to appreciate is that learning is a really broad thing.

Learning is basically how a person organizes their thought processes over time. It's building up resources that they have to call upon to be able to make sense out of what's going on, to make predictions, and solve problems.

So, it really is a value judgement. It depends what you're educating for. What's the purpose of your educational intervention?

Josh: In other words, it depends on what you mean by, "Learning,"?

Mary Helen: Right. What do you mean by, "Learning," so, what kind of learners are you meaning to build?

If you're trying to build excellent, efficient sort of processors, then what you described as the Chinese norm might be a very efficient and effective way to do it.

On the other hand, if you're trying to teach for citizenship, for example, to educate kids who will take action against community problems... or if you're trying to teach for methodological and academic innovation so students are willing to ask difficult questions and then try to answer them... then you need learners to appreciate the open-endedness of certain kinds of problem spaces and be comfortable engaging with that uncertainty in a productive way. In these cases, the "teacher has the answers model" is not the most effective way to teach.

And in fact, in China they're having a lot of problems with students being excellent at academic skills but not great innovators, not highly creative learners. It's a balancing act. You need some of each. You can't just be wandering around following your curiosities with no strategy, no limits or constraints, or no structure, right?

This is my value as someone from an international cultural background, but I think we need students who are capable of becoming aware of their own biases in the learning process and monitoring those. There are times when you really need to learn to efficiently crank out certain kinds of calculations. There are times when you need to be able to notice and say, "Wait. What's the ethical implication of me calculating this thing?" Or me figuring out how to make a nuclear bomb? We need students who can ask themselves, "Is there anything else I should be thinking about here besides the physics?"

Skills such as rote calculating can become building blocks that you need to be able to apply later in the space of broader problems in the world.

If you overly focus on the acquisition of the building blocks, the kids don't have a sense of how to apply those things in the world. If you overly focus on the world, they may notice problems, but have no skills with which to solve the problems. Again, they need to have a balance of both. We need students who are able to steer themselves in an active, strategic, adaptive way depending on the place in which they find themselves, depending on the context and the need of that context.

If they apply certain skills, can they back up and notice when there are ethical implications or there's innovations that are needed? Can they become curious on how to pursue those? Then, once they become curious about something, and they recognize that it's something that's truly interesting and important, can they focus themselves to dig in, pulling up those building block skills?

Ideally learners grow a flexible, adaptive, skilled ability to engage. That also inherently means that there will be individual and cultural variability in what's valued. What people will notice as worthy of or warranting attention and innovation, or what the ethical implications of are for certain kinds of problems, is going to be highly cultural and value driven.

So what you want is students who can use their knowledge and their skills to actually prove and examine their own values, their own assumptions, their own world. And to use what they have as building block skills to innovate and make changes and solve problems when they notice that those problems warrant solving.

Josh: So, probably one of the key things is, as educators, as parents, for us to also be able to engage in that kind of agility ourselves.

Mary Helen: Absolutely. The teacher is someone who is highly skilled in the domain in which the students are learning. But, it's not necessarily owning the answers. The teacher is there as a kind of facilitator to support the students being able to construct the answers.

That's a hugely skilled job because it means injecting information when the student needs it. You don't expect them to reinvent calculus necessarily. So, you need to say, "Ah, you know what you need to know about in this problem space? Let me teach you some math that's going to help you." And you go back to it.

Maintaining a focus on long-term vision

Thinking outside of the content — facts, techniques, skills and details — teachers need to be focused on the kind of people they want students to become. Their intention and direction will inform not just the climate of a class, but the actual neurobiological development of their students. Teachers have the potential to influence the future citizens, employees, leaders and thinkers these students will become.

Josh: What's your advice for those of us who are teaching teachers... and teaching people who teach in the corporate sector... and teaching coaches... and teaching parents? Where do we need to focus to help educators to be able to do to achieve that vision of learning you described earlier?

Mary Helen: I think what we need is the educators have to have a very clear idea of what their goal is, what they want their students to be able to do. And that doesn't just mean what skills they can produce on cue. But it means what kind of person do you want to facilitate these students becoming? What kind of thinker in this domain?

When you have a very clear vision for what high-level thinking and behaving looks like in the domain, then you can sort of step back and support kind of many paths up the mountain. You engage the students and support the students by providing and orchestrating opportunities for them to construct for themselves skills and experiences that will advance them toward that goal.

You're very clear on what the goal is. You're less prescriptive about what the paths are. Some kids are going to scale the cliff, and some are going to take the fire road that's slow and long and meanders through the scenery. And some kids are going to hike up, you know what I'm saying?

Josh: I want to double-click on this thing about vision. A lot of times when people are in this space of learning, they think about the goal of learning, they're kind of caught up in the short term, the test score. I recently had a group of school principals in Japan, and I said to them, "If you're wildly successful, what's going to be happening for your students in 30 years?"

In education, that kind of thinking might be something you do over a beer... but maybe not a formal part of what it means to be an educator.

Mary Helen: It should be a formal part of what it means to be an educator. I mean, I think you've touched on something there. We need to really think seriously – we're in a changing world. Education is an institution that is here to serve our citizens in order to facilitate them and support them in becoming productive members of society.

As society changes, education has to move with it and be a supportive force towards a new kind of world. Towards advancing people toward

> 66
>
> *It is literally neurobiologically impossible to think deeply about things that you don't care about.*
>
> 99

a new kind of citizenship, a new kind of global connectedness, a new way of productivity. And we have to think what the aims of education are so that we're supporting that high level goal.

What kind of people are you supporting these students to become? That has to be always present in the conversation, so that the way in which you're scaffolding, the development of building block skills is at the service of facilitating the development of a particular kind of engaged learner over time. And that goal has to be present in the conversation. But, for so many teachers – and I understand this. I mean, they're so overwhelmed with so little resources and so little support to think this way that they're really narrowed down and focused onto the short-term goal.

Of course, you have to support the development of a short-term goals. A kid has to learn how to add in first grade or whatever. But it's not just so you know how to add, it's so that you know how to think and manipulate things mentally in a way that's appropriate for a kid of that age. And in a way that sets them up to think creatively and in an engaged way without the role of quantity in predicting and understanding the role looking forward. And so, we have to keep that in mind.

Josh: In some ways what you're saying the very kind of conversation you want teachers to be having with students about meaning-making is the same conversation we need to be having among educators.

Mary Helen: Maybe they're on a different developmental level, and the content that they're trying to master is different. But, adults and children are both learners. Actually, learning is co-constructed between them. It's not a property of the teacher or of the student. It's a property of the dynamic cultural context they co-construct.

4.4 Reflecting on the application of Six Seconds Learning Philosophy and latest neuroscience in your classroom

Main Ideas. Summarize the main ideas in the articles you just read (Six Seconds Learning Philosophy, Hallmarks of a great EQ-powered lesson, and Learning about learning and the brain. An interview with Immordino-Yang).

Insights. What did you think while reading the text? What did you feel? Were you surprised, worried, excited, etc.?

Direction. What does this mean for your classroom instruction? What are the practical implications for teaching and learning?

5. Direct Instruction of EQ Competencies

Six Seconds EQ lessons and trainings have a basic, but powerful structure to organize content and activities for meaningful learning. There are three main parts to a great EQ lesson: engage (E), active (A) and reflect (R).

Engage

Here you begin to hook the students, drawing them into the focus of the lesson. Your goal here is to stimulate pre-existing knowledge and establish signposts pointing toward new learning. At the same time, you build interest and emotional connection to the subject matter so they become curious and involved.

Activate

Now that the learners are present, awake, and interested, it's time to bring the content alive. EQ lessons are exercises that provide real-time experience and practice to acquire and develop social and emotional competencies. The goal is to stimulate new insight by jumping into the material.

Reflect

The final step is to pull the learning together and to prepare to apply it. In this phase, through dialogue, journal writing, or other methods of contemplation, students make sense of their new learning and determine how they can put it in action outside your classroom.

5.1 Sample Scope and Sequence for EQ competencies

Competency	Level 1	Level 2	Level 3
Enhance Emotional Literacy	Develop basic feeling vocabulary Identify causes of basic feelings	Expand feeling vocabulary Learn "logic" of feelings; causes & effects	Develop a depth of meaning of feelings and blends Understand sources of conflicting feelings
Recognize Patterns	Become more observant of thoughts, feelings, actions Begin to consider patterns	Sharpen observation skills to become more accurate and realistic Learn to identify patterns immediately following reaction	Increase clarity of recognizing patterns in the moment and over longer time periods Learn about group patterns
Apply Consequential Thinking	Learn about costs and benefits Begin to assess immediate consequences	Increase skill in assessing results of choices Become aware of effects of emotions	Increase ability to evaluate choices and results Predict consequences of feelings
Navigate Emotions	Become more aware of sensing emotions Recognize that it is possible to change feelings	Increase ability to shift or change feelings Develop multiple strategies for changing feelings	Learn to generate emotions to motivate effective action Increase awareness of 2-way influence of feelings and thoughts

Competency	Level 1	Level 2	Level 3
Exercise Optimism	Increase awareness of multiple choices/ options Learn to realistically appraise risk	Learn PPP-TIE* framework for optimistic response Increase capacity to reframe pessimistic explanations	Become more able to generate positive emotion Learn that adversity is an opportunity for growth
Engage Intrinsic Motivation	Define motivation Recognize influence of seeking extrinsic reward	Learn to recognize intrinsic vs. extrinsic motivators Strengthen internal motivators	Become aware that personal choice leads to self-efficacy Increase capacity to resist external pressure/ conformity
Increase Empathy	Become more curious about others Recognize shared concerns and experiences	Become more accurate in identifying emotional cues Increase respect for others	Practice and internalize empathic response See effect of empathy in relationships
Pursue Noble Goals	Recognize that people live in communities Increase perception of self-efficacy	Expand sphere of concern Become aware of interdependence	Develop principles and ethical thinking Increase commitment to take action based on principles

*PPP= Permanent, pervasive, personal; TIE = Temporary, Isolated, Event-driven.

5.2 Six Seconds Lesson Template

Over the years, we have developed a lesson and activity template that works well for most curriculum writers, teachers and schools, and even universities writing SEL lessons or infusing EQ competencies in academic instruction. See lesson template on page 80.

In the second line of the template, lesson writers may list academic standards and other SEL standards that apply. The objectives line of the template allows you, the writer, to summarize what you want your learners to learn from the activity. In the Big Questions line, write a powerful question that you would like your students to think about and be able to discuss at the end of the lesson.

The Six Seconds EQ competencies are represented in the next line, with the option to choose one or more that will be directly taught or infused into the lesson.

In the Session plan, the Engage, Activate, Reflect structure is critical to lesson creation; as a reminder, here the phases are explained in more detail.

Engage: Create cognitive and emotional hooks to create interest, activate pre-existing knowledge, and develop a context for new learning. Blend emotion, physical activity, creativity, and powerful questions to create "hot cognition" to activate the brain for learning. In this phase, students become curious and want to know more.

Activate: Build capability and enroll the brain through real-time experiences that blend the emotional and cognitive content. Bring powerful mental models to life so participants can begin to learn and test out new concepts. Bring it alive using multiple senses. Make the learning real through projects and experiences that make new concepts personally meaningful. In this phase, new insights are stimulated by jumping in to the material.

Reflect: Integrate new learning by synthesizing and concluding, so this knowledge, attitudes, and skills can be more readily applied. Invite the participants to pull it together and commit to next steps; create choice, ask powerful questions, be curious as a facilitator. In this phase, through dialogue, journal writing, or other methods of reflection, student make sense of their new learning and determine how they can put it in action outside of the classroom.

Try it out for yourself in your next lesson. What do you think?

School
Grade(s)/Level(s):

LESSON TITLE	
COMPETENCY	
OBJECTIVE(S)	
UNIVERSAL THEME(S)*	
LEARNING PHILOSOPHY PRINCIPLE(S)	
***BIG* QUESTIONS**	
Length of session	30 minutes (any activities that will take longer than 30 min. should be included in extensions)
Materials Needed	

SESSION PLAN:

ENGAGE (Draw them in with emotion, data, and a substantive model or framework)
ACTIVATE (Bring it alive and make it real)
REFLECT (invite the participants to pull it together and commit to the next steps).

ASSESSMENT

EXTENSIONS

HOME-SCHOOL CONNECTION

NOTES/VARIATIONS

*See universal themes and their definitions in the next page.

> 66
>
> *Engage: Prepare the brain for learning*
>
> *Activate: Bring insights to life*
>
> *Reflect: Find meaning, take action*
>
> 99

Universal Themes

We recognize there are issues in the world that need solving. These universal themes are for the teacher more than for the students. We live in a multicultural world. In every classroom, we have diversity in race, language, gender, special needs, and sexual orientation.

Living in a digital world

The world is rapidly changing through technology and we are all impacted by it. It is important to help students to safely navigate the challenges and rewards of the internet, and the use of digital technology to access information, learn and collaborate together. The impact of social media in youth's lives cannot be overestimated and should be addressed in the classroom.

Equity, diversity, and inclusion

Equity - Creating opportunities for all students to have equal access to and participate in educational programs, which, in turn, may help all students achieve.

Diversity - Individual differences and social differences in the school community are recognized and promoted in the service of learning.

Inclusion - The active and intentional process of working with diversity in the school community to increase individual and group awareness, understanding, and empathy, and access and equal participation in learning.

Cultural relevance

Our cultures influence our perspective. In a global world where cross-cultural or multicultural experiences are prevalent and necessary for the 21st century, teachers are aware of their own perspective, help the class make meaning within their students' own cultural context, and at the same time, help students embrace a wider view of culture.

Global citizenship

A Global Citizen is someone who: is aware of the wider world and has a sense of their own role as a world citizen (Oxfam). A global citizen is a responsible, open-minded, and compassionate human being and seeks ways to contribute to a better world. "I want my world to be centered on what makes a better world and how can I contribute to that."

Social and environmental justice

Issues that impact the planet impact people as well; social and environmental concerns are interrelated. From a community scale to a global scale there is an intense connection between people and the Earth, and harm to one cannot be escaped by the other (Pachamama Alliance). "The empathy card is always appropriate to play for oneself, for one's colleagues, for one's community, and for the earth".

5.3 Sample Lesson: I am a Bucket Filler!

School: Synapse

Grade level: 1st and 2nd grade

LESSON TITLE	Empathy Frogs
COMPETENCY	Empathy
OBJECTIVE(S)	Predicts how others are feeling based on their facial expressions and body language. Tool= E(mpathy)-motion (action)
UNIVERSAL THEME(S)	Equity, diversity and inclusion
LEARNING PHILOSOPHY PRINCIPLE(S)	Emotions Drive People 1, 2, 3, Pasta!
BIG QUESTIONS	How can we put our bodies into "motion" in support of other people who need us?
Length of session	30 minutes
Materials Needed	• Projector and speakers to show this Youtube video: ▪ https://www.YouTube.com/watch?v=xdeuivQYnas • Class set of Origami instruction sheets (provided at back of lesson) • Class set of the paper in the instructions or can use 4" x 6" cardstock • Completed sample "frog" for each pair of students to unfold and copy • Markers/pencils/pens to customize act of kindness message (and designs on frog) • *Optional:* music to play while students work; blue poster board "pond"

SESSION PLAN:

ENGAGE (VIDEO) 5 min

Write these questions on the board and speak to the students as you write:

- What do the boys observe?
- How do the boys feel?
- What do the boys do?

Tell the students that they will watch a video and say, "Watch for ways these boys responded to another boy's being bullied."

Show video: https://www.YouTube.com/watch?v=xdeuivQYnas

Ask the students for their answers to the questions on the board. Now add one more question to the board:

- What can we do here in our class and at our school?

Prompt the students to generate a list of positive acts they can do at their school and write them in a list where all students can see. Tell students:

"Empathy is when we notice how others are feeling and respond appropriately. The word emotion has the *motion* inside of it. Motions are actions. Today you are going to work together to put your bodies into motion in support of other people who need you."

ACTIVATE (FROG ORIGAMI) 20-25 min

Separate the students into pairs. Hand out one pattern, one instruction sheet, and one sample frog per pair, or have student helpers do this. Have students decide on and use pencils, pens, or markers to write one of the kind acts from the board onto their frog, then fold it up, and test hop.

Circulate and listen, praise and encourage deeper discussions. Help students understand any challenging folding instructions. You could turn on upbeat and inspirational music while students work to fold their origami.

If time allows, create a lily pond out of blue poster board and let the pairs "hop" their frogs off their desks and into the pond creating ripples of kindness in the classroom and around the school.

Tell students to clean up the supplies and either place their frogs into a box for storage or leave them in the pond.

REFLECT (DISCUSSION) 5 min

Bring students back to single focus. Ask them:

- What did you notice?

- How did you feel?

- In what ways did you help your partner?

- Was it easy or hard to decide on a message to put inside the frog? Why?

- How can we put our bodies into "motion" in support of other people who need us?

- If you had a sheet of paper, what message could you fold and send to build community spirit? What ongoing activities could you initiate? (ex: frog-a-thons, ...)

CLASSROOM ASSESSMENT

Students submit their frog pairs to teacher as demonstration of learning. Teacher observes during discussion and partner work. Students could describe one way they will help or include someone new this week.

EXTENSIONS

- Create a chart or calendar to help students see how they are adding to the good in their community.

- Break students into teams based on gender to discuss inclusion among friend groups.

- Read chapters from How to Beat the Bully *Without Really Trying* by Scott Starkey.

- Discuss bystanders and upstanders.

HOME-SCHOOL CONNECTION

Provide extra copies of the frog origami template for students to take home to their families. Encourage students to brainstorm with their families more ideas for using empathy to support others in need.

Students can report back what they discussed at home with their families and add to a classroom poster of "empathy in action".

NOTES/VARIATIONS

Special education students

Pair students with manual challenges with others with slightly stronger fine motor skills. If students have emotional challenges (patience required with folding) provide pre-folded papers and pair with students who they can talk through the video with and focus on decorating. If the student has an aide, provide materials for both.

Gifted or advanced students

If students finish their frogs very quickly, encourage them to design a new shape or origami symbol to accompany the frogs in the pond (ex: a lily pad, flies, fish, etc.). What could these new symbols represent? What kindness could they bring to the community? Challenge students to brainstorm more ways that they can put their empathy into motion in ways that have not been written on the board. Students can use books or movies they have seen as areas of inspiration. Also, you could challenge students with inventing a kindness test or formula to write on their new origami designs.

5.4 Teachers' Ratings of Students' Social and Emotional Competencies

The following observation tool can help you identify how often students in your classroom practice the competencies in the Six Seconds model. This tool can be used several times during the school year; for example, you could observe your students after teaching several SEL lessons or before you have to turn in report cards.

Once you collect these data, think about students' individual strengths and their areas of growth. What is one thing you could do to help them grow their skills? Also, look for trends in the classroom. Are there any specific skills that your classroom as a whole would benefit from further developing? Could you incorporate these skills in your academic lessons?

Student Name: _____

Date of Observation: _____

Think about your student's behavior over the past 3 weeks and indicate *how often* you see the student display each of the behaviors below. Rarely (R), occasionally (O), frequently (F), almost always (AA)

	Know Yourself - Self-awareness (EL – RP)
	1. Understands his or her own strengths or weaknesses.
	2. Is able to explain why he or she said or did something
	3. Expresses feelings that are appropriate to the situation
	4. Is comfortable sharing feelings in a culturally appropriate way
	5. Is able to identify reactions or repetitive behaviors and habits
	6. Is able to change/modify typical reactions or behaviors
	Choose Yourself - Self-management (CT – NE – IM – EO)
	1. Follows classroom rules.
	2. Can control his or her behavior when angry, frustrated, disappointed, or excited
	3. Is able to see alternatives facing problems
	4. Stays on task even with distractions
	5. Can evaluate costs and benefits of choices
	6. Can move towards goals based on internal rewards
	Give Yourself – Self-direction (IE – PNG)
	1. Resolves disputes or peer pressure constructively
	2. Takes responsibility for his/her own actions.
	3. Align daily choices with purpose and principles
	4. Respects other people's viewpoints.
	5. Works well with others
	6. Responds with empathy to others who are upset.

EL = Enhance Emotional Literacy
CT = Apply Consequential Thinking
IM = Engage Intrinsic Motivation
IE = Increase Empathy

RP = Recognize Patterns
NE = Navigate Emotions
EO = Exercise Optimism
PNG = Pursue Noble Goals.

This grid is meant for k12 teachers. Adapted with permission from CASEL, 2013.

5.5 *I Do, We Do, You Do*

By Lorea Martinez, Ph.D.

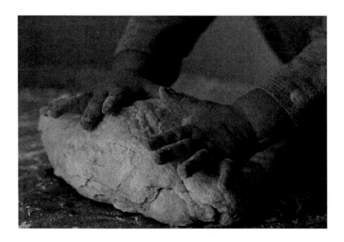

"Mama! Remember... You cannot say stupid". My 4-year old daughter does not let me forget that she is watching and learning from the way I behave, what I say and how I relate to others. As a parent, I need to be able to *model* the behaviors and skills that I expect her to develop and practice on a regular basis. As you have probably experienced at some point, children and youth are watching adult behavior all the time, and they often feel puzzled when we ask them to do things they don't see adults doing. Intentionally or not, adults model social and emotional skills for children and youth.

This is especially relevant for educators. As I explain in further detail in the Edutopia article *Developing Teachers' Social and Emotional Skills*, teachers navigate stressful situations every day – and students are paying attention. They learn from how their teachers manage frustration, deal with conflicts, or maintain control in the classroom. Although as human beings we are not perfect and we often make mistake, being aware of the impact our behavior has on our students can help us make different

> *Think about your classroom. When and how do you model positive social and emotional skills?*

choices if necessary. Think about your classroom. When and how do you model positive social and emotional skills?

Let's say that you want to develop your students' self-management skills, so they can regulate their emotions and respond (instead of react) to difficult situations in and out of the classroom. You would need to model the skills by anticipating your reactions to students' behavior, pausing to consider your choices before taking action or acknowledging mistakes when your behavior choices were not that great. In Gandhi's words: "*Be the change you wish to see in the world*"!

Although modeling is very important to teach SEL in schools, it is not enough to develop students' social and emotional skills. You will need to set aside some time to teach these skills explicitly. An effective teaching strategy to explicitly teach SEL skills is "I Do, We Do, You Do". It incorporates the 3 key components of skill development: modeling, guided practice and independent application. Following the example of teaching students self-management skills, here's how you could use the strategy in the classroom.

I Do – This phase involves teaching strategies such as *informing, explaining, modeling* and *providing examples*. You could:

- Introduce and explain effective tools to regulate emotions. For example, taking a few deep breaths, moving your body or moving away from the difficult situation. You could also have students brainstorm ideas.

- Model how to use the tools. You would do a few breathing exercises with your students or model how to move away from a difficult situation in a constructive way.

- Provide examples from your personal or professional life and how you regulated your emotions (successfully or not).

We Do – This second phase involves *practicing* the skills and tools with your students. It is important to create a space where students feel comfortable and safe practicing the tools; if they don't feel at ease, it is better to spend more time creating the right atmosphere in the classroom than plowing ahead with the guided practice. Since for some students this might be the first time they are practicing these tools, continue to model for them and provide feedback as necessary. Help students make sense of these tools. You could:

- Role-play difficult situations, have students choose which tool seems more appropriate and discuss outcomes.

- Discuss scenes with strong emotions from books or movies. Did the characters use any tools to regulate their emotions? Did it work?

- Have students lead the guided practice. For example, students could lead breathing exercises.

You Do – This phase involves the student practicing the tools independently. At the beginning of teaching self-management tools,

> 66
>
> *Although modeling is very important to teach SEL in schools, it is not enough to develop students' social and emotional skills. You will need to set aside some time to teach these skills explicitly.*
>
> 99

students might need reminders to breath or take a break when they are in the midst of a difficult situation. Over time and with on-going practice, students will be able to use these tools independently both inside and outside the classroom. During this phase, it is important that you provide feedback and monitor when/how students are using these tools. You could:

- Observe how students handle classroom conflict. Do they use any of the self-regulation tools you taught them?

- Analyze your classroom behavior data. Do you notice any differences and/or patterns? How can this data inform your future SEL lessons?

- Check-in with other teachers and school staff that work with your students. Do they observe them using these tools successfully?

As with teaching academic content, if after independent practice, students are not applying the tools, you would go back to the "We Do" phase and provide additional guided practice. This additional check-in with students can also provide an opportunity to celebrate successes and discuss the challenges students encounter when using these tools.

You can bring SEL to your classroom by consistently modeling the behaviors you expect to see in your students and by teaching these skills explicitly to your students. The strategy "I Do, We Do, You Do" is a great way to organize your SEL lessons, so your students can learn from you, have opportunities to practice together in a safe place and apply the skills independently with your feedback. Give it a try and let me know how it goes!

Originally published in Social Emotional Learning and the Common Core blog by Lorea Martinez, Ph.D.

> *What is your goal for learning?*
>
> *Is knowledge enough, or does learning also require meaning-making?*
>
> *Is meaning enough, or does learning also require action?*

6. Integrating EQ with Teaching Practices

6.1 *Structuring Transformational Learning*

By Joshua Freedman

What is your goal with learning? Is it enough for participants to get information, or do you want some change, some transformation, as they actually APPLY the learning?

What makes that work?

One the reasons Six Seconds' programs are transformational is our commitment to a rigorous approach to learning. We come from a "constructivist" history, rooted in the humanistic school of education. In constructivism, the goal is for learners to build (construct) meaning. Rather than imparting information or telling them what you've just taught, a constructivist focuses on facilitating learners to answer their own questions and to integrate new insights. We are also influenced by "confluent" theory, the notion that richness in learning comes from the flowing together of cognition and emotion.

In recent decades, "brain-based learning" captures these schools of thought and advocates for learning that builds "hot cognition." Hot cognition means there is a highly activated brain state where thinking is accelerated and deepened because the learner is fully involved. I've posted before about our learning philosophy, the five principles we use to guide the way we teach, coach, facilitate, mentor, and consult so that we fuel hot cognition — this is the "how" of our methodology.

In addition to that underlying "how," we have a very specific design methodology which structures learning as a change process. Because learning and change are so closely linked, we use our Change MAP as a structure (a good orientation to this model can be seen in the Case Study about our change program with the US Navy). As we apply the change process to learning, we get a very powerful structure.

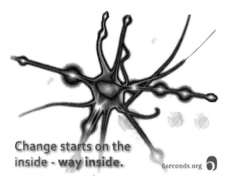

Change starts on the inside - way inside.

6seconds.org

The Change MAP, and our learning design method, is a spiraling cycle. There are three phases which we present in a circle to emphasize the fact that learning (and change) require numerous iterations. In the MAP, you can see the critically important "red lines," the emotional transitions required to accelerate change. These same transitions are essential for learning, because if we don't get emotional connection, we don't get hot cognition. The three phases are:

- **Engage**: Create cognitive and emotional hooks to create interest, activate pre-existing knowledge, and develop a context for new learning. At the end of this phase, participants should see the value of the subject matter and be ready for more.

- **Activate**: Build capability and enroll the brain through real-time experiences that blend emotional and cognitive content; bring powerful mental models to life so participants can begin to learn and test out new concepts. At the end of this phase, participants will have new knowledge plus a "gut level" experience of the concept.

- **Reflect**: Integrate new learning by synthesizing and concluding, so this knowledge, attitudes, and skills can be more readily applied. At the end of this phase, participants should know what they've learned and a commitment to put that into action.

Iterative Cycles

These phases apply equally to a twenty-minute module, a 90-minute keynote, a five-day workshop – or a three-month development program (which will include hundreds of iterations of this cycle within one large "meta cycle" spanning the program).

Next Up

How can you use it? Whether you're a trainer, teacher, coach, operations leader, HR professional, parent, or friend you can use this framework for learning. Where do you want to make learning stick? What would happen if you structured the process more carefully so your group (and you) can take in new info and actually make meaning? Think about the next keynote you're giving, the next meeting you're facilitating, the next car ride where you're chatting. How can you build momentum with these phases?

- **Engage**: Draw them in with emotion, data, and a substantive model or framework.

- **Activate**: Bring it alive and make it real.

- **Reflect**: Invite the participants to pull it together and commit to the next steps.

Then do it again!

Originally published at 6seconds.org

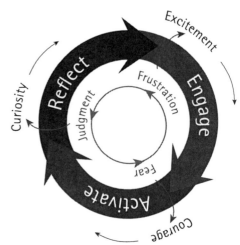

6.2 Reflecting to Learn

By Lorea Martinez, Ph.D.

I recently came across the book "The 5 Dimensions of Engaged Teaching", a practical approach to teaching and learning that focuses on meaning, purpose and motivation in the classroom and incorporates social and emotional competencies. One of the practices in the model is **engaging the self-observer**, which the authors Weaver and Wilding (2013) define as cultivating the ability to notice, observe, and then reflect on our thoughts, beliefs, biases, emotions, and actions to make more conscious choices.

This principle asks students and teachers alike to acknowledge their feelings, thoughts, and actions in order to make better, more conscious  decisions, instead of functioning on autopilot. In the classroom, it might translate into creating time and spaces for reflection and self-analysis. This reflective practice, if build as part of a daily routine, will develop students' self-awareness and self-management, but also help them make sense of their learning. Dewey (1962) claimed that we don't learn from experience, we learn from reflecting on experience. Reflecting helps us to clarify what was learned and, hopefully, it will inspire new thoughts and actions.

Engaging in reflective practices becomes even more necessary now as educators and students transition to the Common Core. Being a critical thinker, which is highlighted in the standards, involves being an active observer, asking pertinent questions, evaluating arguments and being open to examine own beliefs and assumptions (and change one's mind!). Most of those skills require being able to stop and observe, study and think, and also wonder. Building time and space for reflection about our thoughts and feelings, and what we have learned, will help students and colleagues to make more conscious decisions and be ready to develop new learning.

Reflective activities will vary depending on the audience, the desired outcome or the amount of time available. These are just a few examples that can be incorporated in the classroom:

- **Journaling.** Students (and educators) may record activities, thoughts, feelings and questions in an individual or group journal. Depending on the desired outcome, you could ask students to reflect on the day, what they wish to accomplish or what they have learned. This could also be a time for free writing. Journaling works really well to help students focus after recess or lunch, but it can also be used at the end of the day or following an activity.

- **Group discussion.** Listening and speaking are also ways to reflect, and they enhance students' social and emotional competencies. You can facilitate discussions focused on the content and skills that students are learning in your class, address classroom concerns or build a sense of community. These shared spaces can assist learners to make sense of their learning and the learning of others.

- **Portfolios.** Essentially portfolios are a collection of pieces from a learning experience. They help students make connections among interests and skills, and how they relate to what they are learning in school. Portfolios bring a great opportunity for students to reflect on their strengths, and how they could use them to accomplish their goals. Digital portfolios, such as slide shows or multimedia presentations, provide a forum for students to both construct the fruits of knowledge while simultaneously reflecting on it.

- **Art.** Some students might prefer to express their feelings or thoughts visually rather than verbally or in writing. Offer students the chance to draw or paint, especially for younger students, as a way to reflect about themselves and their learning.

These opportunities for reflection should occur, when possible, before, during and after key activities or events in the classroom. We want students to develop self-awareness and self-management skills by encouraging  reflection of their starting point and their progress, and by allowing students to evaluate their own learning. Incorporating reflective activities like the ones described here into your teaching practices will develop students' social and emotional competencies and will help students consolidate what they know so new learning can take place.

Originally published in Social Emotional Learning and the Common Core blog by Lorea Martinez, Ph.D.

6.3 Design Thinking: Empathy is a Design Mindset (part 1 and 2)

By Lorea Martinez, Ph.D.

 Melissa Pelochino is the Director of Professional Development at the K12 Lab, Stanford University Design School, known as the d.school. She plays at the intersection of design thinking and K12 education. We talked about design thinking, empathy and the connections between the two. Follow her on Twitter @ mpelochino.

Martinez: Many schools are now adopting the design thinking process as a way to teach and increase student engagement. Can you tell us what design thinking is?

Pelochino: Design thinking started as a methodology used by designers to solve complex problems, and it has steadily moved into other domains like business and education for some time now. At the most basic level, design thinking is thought of as a 5-step process. The first step is to empathize, which is getting into other people's shoes... literally! Interviewing people, observing them or immersing yourself in what they do. The second step is to define, which is when designers identify implicit needs that users have, or reframe a problem in a new way. The third step is to ideate, which is when designers brainstorm novel solutions to the problems or opportunities they have identified. The fourth step is to prototype, that is making ideas tangible, often with few resources. The last step is to test, which is inviting users to experience your solution and having them help you make it better.

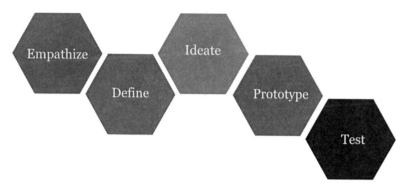

Below the surface of these steps, there are certain design principles, which we refer to as mindsets... this is where I personally think all the fun is! Design mindsets normally emerge only after having gone through the design thinking process many times.

Martinez: Can you share a few of these design mindsets?

Pelochino: For example, one principle is having an empathetic mindset, which means that you are always looking for multiple and diverse points of view before you make decisions about a problem. Another principle is to have a bias towards action, which is having an idea and doing something about it. Another principle is identifying and challenging assumptions, which is being aware that there are norms accepted as "truth" and challenging them. When designers begin to take on these mindsets, their way of working and their way of being starts to transform... it's super powerful.

Martinez: Why are so many schools using design thinking?

Pelochino: With the adoption of the Common Core Standards, process-based learning is finally moving to the forefront in our education system. Schools are excited about having a process which promotes critical thinking and rigorous discourse in the classroom. Educators are thrilled about using the process at school-wide or district-wide levels as well, not only in the classroom. There are just so many opportunities to make our current education system better and this process is an amazing lever for change.

Martinez: Empathy seems to be at the core of design thinking. Why is empathy so important?

Pelochino: Empathy is the foundation of design thinking. We find that most people naturally design for themselves simply because they don't have a process to help them to "get out" of their own head. We are inherently biased and this creates many problems... people get very attached to their ideas, whether they work or not. They often spend lots of time and money on these ideas, and get emotionally involved. This is not conducive to powerful problem solving. Using a process like design thinking helps designers to get into the lives and experiences of others. It helps them be less focused on their *own* emotions and more focused on what is actually needed. People don't need to spend time arguing about ideas in meetings; generally speaking, the solutions either work or they don't.

Martinez: Can you describe some strategies that you use to develop empathy?

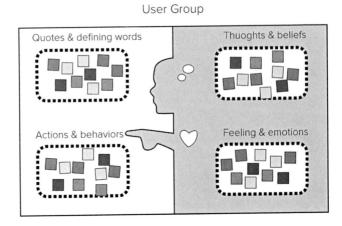

User Group

Pelochino: There are three meaningful ways to develop empathy for others. One way is through interviewing, where you have conversations with your end users. It's an overlooked and undervalued way to develop empathy, but it is extremely effective. Another way to develop empathy is through observation; we find that what people say, and what people do, don't always line up. Through observation, designers can pick up on these discrepancies. A third way to develop empathy is by immersing yourself in other people's' experiences. For example, if you are redesigning the cafeteria for your school, you would stand in line, get your tray, etc. so you could see for yourself what your users are experiencing. This is a meaningful way to develop empathy!

Martinez: What are some of your designers' reactions to these activities?

Pelochino: Participants are often surprised by what they notice. We make a lot of assumptions about day-to-day living; we don't notice a lot of details in our surroundings. Designers often uncover new perspectives after going through these empathy exercises. Observing, interviewing and immersing are only the first steps in the empathy work. The rest of the work includes interpreting what you see, hear, and experience, and making some leaps about what it all means.

Martinez: From an SEL perspective, we say that empathy starts with knowing who you are, because that allows you to connect with others at an emotional level. How do you think that design thinking helps students and teachers be more self-aware?

Pelochino: I think it's a cyclical process. If you know yourself better, you are able to tap into other people in a more powerful way. By tapping into other people's perspectives and seeing their point of view, you can continue to refine who you are. Design thinking creates this cycle of learning, where by immersing yourself into other people's experiences, you learn to uncover more about yourself. Also, any process-based learning requires metacognition. The scientific method, the writing process and design thinking all require that you are intentional about what you do and why you do it. As a result, people become more aware and thoughtful about their behaviors.

Martinez: How do you think that design thinking and SEL can support each other to improve teaching and learning?

Pelochino: Designers very often try to tap into the emotions of the users for whom they are creating solutions, and we use many strategies in order to do this. One example is a strategy called "why laddering", where you ask the question "why" several times in a row. After asking "why" four or five times, answers tend to be less based on facts or thoughts, and more based on feelings. Participants will say things like "because it makes me feel happy" or "because I feel more in control". Once designers get to this important emotional information, they can start designing solutions to replicate these emotions.

Martinez: Design thinkers need to be open and leave any judgments behind in order to fully listen and "tune into" their users' experiences. What could educators do to embrace this mindset?

Pelochino: Designing for others is an act of kindness and fidelity; trust in the design thinking process will help designers to focus on what matters most, the people for whom they are designing. The d.school, in partnership with IDEO, has just launched the Shadow a Student Challenge as part of the School Retool project, which will take place at the end of this month. It's a crash course on empathy and it's free! Some other great resources available are the d.school's method cards and IDEO's Design Thinking for Educators Toolkit.

In our next post, Empathy is a Design Mindset part 2, we will discuss practical ways to develop empathy the "design thinking" way.

Originally published in Social Emotional Learning and the Common Core blog by Lorea Martinez, Ph.D.

Empathy is a Design Mindset - Part 2

Empathy is the ability to be understanding of and sensitive to another person's feelings and thoughts without having had the same experience. In an earlier post, Pelochino described empathy as the foundation of design thinking. Innovators and designers develop a deep emotional understanding of people's needs, and they use this knowledge to address complex problems. How can empathy be developed in classrooms and schools?

IDEO, a global design firm that uses a human-centered approach to help organizations innovate and grow, recommends making empathy in design a deliberate practice. That is to say, being *intentional* about creating opportunities to connect with people in meaningful ways, and setting aside reactions and behaviors that might interfere with this process. Using design thinking with students to solve challenges can be a great way to make empathy an intentional practice in classrooms. The strategies used in the design thinking process develop three different kinds of empathy (cognitive, emotional and compassionate) in an intentional way. Let's take a look!

1. **Meaningful interviews** help designers understand a person's thoughts, emotions, and motivations. During the interview process innovators develop cognitive empathy, which is knowing how the other person feels and what they might be thinking, also known as *perspective-taking*. Goleman describes cognitive empathy as mind-to-mind understanding; it tells us how best to communicate with that person, what matters most to them or their worldviews. If you are running a design challenge in your classroom, for example,

> **"**
>
> *Empathy fuels motivation and creative problem-solving; it helps people to think beyond themselves and deepen their understanding of the human experience.*
>
> **"**

prepare your students by discussing strategies that will help them conduct a productive interview, and by reviewing the social and emotional skills involved in the process (what does active listening look like? What can you do if you notice getting frustrated or becoming judgmental with your interviewee?).

2. **Observing and shadowing** the people for whom you are designing are good strategies to develop empathy. Pelochino reminded us that *"what people say and what they do, don't always line up"*. Finding these discrepancies can give designers great insights into the challenges they are trying to solve. In this case, designers go beyond understanding someone's point of view; they become well-attuned with the other person's emotional world... they feel *with* them. This is what we call emotional empathy, which takes place when you feel physically along with the other person. When you develop this kind of empathy, you will most likely be aware of your body's emotional signals (self-awareness), which mirror the other person's feelings. For example, you might feel the urge to cry when someone else is crying. Emotional empathy can be fueled through becoming someone else for a day. What would happen if you became a student for a day? Join the Shadow a Student Challenge from School Retool, if you want to find out!

3. Another effective way to develop empathy is **immersing yourself in people's experiences**. It means doing what they do, and most importantly, feeling what they feel. Are they stressed, scared or overwhelmed? As we have discussed

> *Using design thinking with students to solve challenges can be a great way to make empathy an intentional practice in classrooms.*

in earlier posts, there is great wisdom in our emotions and it is worth spending some time exploring their meaning. In many cases, when designers immerse themselves in people's experiences, they are moved to take action and help. This is what we call compassionate empathy: we understand this person's perspective, feel with them and are inclined to do something about their needs. Goleman describes compassionate empathy as *heart-to-heart connection;* we feel with others and want to do something to improve their experiences. If you are designing for your students, ask yourself "what would I do differently to improve their experience?" and "what emotions would I want them to feel instead of...?".

Empathy fuels motivation and creative problem-solving; it helps people to think beyond themselves and deepen their understanding of the human experience. Engaging in design thinking can help your classroom and school develop cognitive, emotional and compassionate empathy in an intentional way. Give it a try and let us know how it goes!

Originally published in Social Emotional Learning and the Common Core blog by Lorea Martinez, Ph.D.

6.4 Integrating EQ in your Classroom

New ideas. What are some new things you'd like to try in your classroom based on what you read in this chapter?

Challenges. What are some challenges you anticipate having when implementing these new ideas? What can you do to overcome them? Who can help you?

Next Steps. What are your immediate next steps to bring EQ to your classroom or after-school program?

> *Perseverance, along with grit and tenacity, has been recognized as essential to an individual's capacity to succeed at long-term goals, and to persist in the face of challenges and obstacles.*

7. Integrating EQ with Academic Content

7.1 *Perseverance in Solving Problems*

By Lorea Martinez, Ph.D.

The Mathematics Common Core Standards outline certain mathematical practices that students should develop in class. The first practice is "Make sense of problems and persevere in solving them"; this means that students need to be able to make sense of the information in a problem through different approaches, select a process for solving the problem and explain why it makes sense, as well as use alternative approaches when necessary. This practice moves away from "quickly getting the right answer" to focus on the process through which a solution can be drawn. But how do we teach perseverance to students?

Perseverance, along with grit and tenacity, has been recognized as essential to an individual's capacity to succeed at long-term goals, and to persist in the face of challenges and obstacles. Researchers have been highlighting for a few years now the impact that these non-cognitive skills can have on students; some of the best-known scholars are Carol Dweck and her research on growth mindset (2006), as well as Angela Duckworth and her work on grit (2007). A recent report (Shechtman et al., 2013) highlights the common findings in research related to perseverance, grit and tenacity, which have direct implications for teaching and learning:

1. Learning environments can be designed to promote grit, tenacity and perseverance. This means that educators provide opportunities for students to take on goals that are challenging,

but within students' range of proximal development (not too easy or too difficult). Educators should help students connect these goals with their values and interests, so students become intrinsically motivated to accomplish these objectives. At the same time, in order for students to pursue these challenging goals, the classroom climate should regard making mistakes and struggling as part of the learning process, and effort should be emphasized over ability. The bottom line is that you want students to feel safe making mistakes and taking risks, and feel supported in this process of struggling with challenging goals.

2. Students can develop psychological resources that promote grit, tenacity and perseverance. Research has shown that social and emotional competencies are malleable and can be learned (and taught!) over time. One of the aspects that often holds students back in their math work is not based on their knowledge of math concepts or procedures, but their academic mindsets. The beliefs, mindsets, attitudes, dispositions or ways of perceiving oneself can have a powerful impact on performance and how students react in the face of challenge. One of these mindsets is Dweck's growth mindset: "My ability and competence grow with my effort". You can actually test your mindset on-line and for free by accessing Dweck's website Mindset. Exploring your students' beliefs about their abilities and competencies, and addressing them in the classroom, will help you be more effective and help students learn better and be more motivated. In addition to considering students' academic mindsets in your instruction, there is a second element that will help students persevere in the face of challenges: having specific strategies to deal with difficulties. You can develop a list of strategies with your students for "what to do when you feel stuck" and post it in your classroom, so students have easy access to this information as they are working on their math problems or other activities. The same process of developing this list with students will

highlight that making mistakes is okay and that we often need to use an alternative approach to solve problems.

Developing perseverance in your students is not an easy task or something that will happen right away, but there are things that you can do to help students persist in the face of challenges: First, create a classroom climate that supports students taking on challenging goals where mistakes are seen as normal to the learning process; second, develop a growth mindset in your students by teaching that intelligence is not fixed, and provide with specific strategies that students can use when they feel stuck. By addressing both the learning environment and students' individual resources you will be helping students develop perseverance and you'll be providing the foundation for great learning!

Originally published in Social Emotional Learning and the Common Core blog by Lorea Martinez, Ph.D.

7.2 Teaching SEL in Math: 2y + 3x = SEL

By Lorea Martinez, Ph.D.

It has been almost 6 years since the Common Core State Standards were released. The adoption of common standards in the US has brought exciting changes for students and teachers, and a fair amount of frustration, anger and fear of failure. Although the standards have received many criticisms, Montoy-Wilson, a 2nd grade teacher in East Palo Alto (California), describes them as a tool to address the achievement gap and equip all students with proper tools for the 21st century:

> **66**
>
> *Every day as I teach the Common Core standards, I am confident and excited that I am equipping my students with habits of mind that will make them college-and-career ready.*
>
> **99**

In Mathematics, the Common Core standards reflect the view that **learning is a social process**, implicitly calling for teaching practices that leverage the power of group work and collaborative learning. The Standards for Mathematical Practice (known as SMPs) require that students solve real-world problems by working effectively with peers; elaborating and communicating arguments; understanding and critiquing diverse points of view;

and persevering in solving problems. Those skills seem to go beyond being able to fill out some bubble sheets, right? **In order to develop students that are mathematically proficient in the Common Core standards, math instruction will need to incorporate the development of** social and emotional competencies.

The Charles A. Dana Center and CASEL have recently published a set of resources connecting the SMPs with the specific SEL competencies that support them. **This is the most comprehensive list of resources that I have seen so far**, and it is definitely worth spending some time going through it. A great place to start is looking at the social and emotional skills that students will need in order to be proficient under the Common Core standards. Here's an example.

Standards for Mathematical Practice 1: ***Make sense of problems and persevere in solving them.***

Expectations	Students' Work	Connection to social and emotional competencies
Students will make sense of the information in a problem through different approaches. *Students will identify alternative ways to solve complex problems.*	Students will try to explain the meaning of the problem and look for entry points to the solution. They will find different pathways to solve the problem, using a variety of tools: concrete objects, graphs, pictures, etc. Students will check their answers and continuously ask "does this make sense?". They will be able to explain the different approaches and why/how they are relevant.	***Self-awareness***: they'll need to know their strengths and what they know about the topic. They'll need to know their existing resources and when to ask for help. If they get stuck, they'll need to exercise optimism. ***Self-management***: they'll need to regulate their behavior and avoid distractions. They'll need to monitor their progress, considering time and effort to meet their goal.

As you can see, in order to prepare students to meet the expectations laid out in the SMP-1 (making sense of problems and persevering in solving them), you will need to support the development of students' self-awareness and self-management skills. Here's how you can do it:

1. **Discuss with your students their** emotional reaction **to math problems.** Do they get excited about the subject or shut down? What's their stress level in your class? If the emotions generated by the subject are not conducive to productive work, you will need to offer alternative ways to think about the subject. How is math connected with the outside world? How can math help them meet their goals?

2. **Help students identify their strengths.** This is the foundation of self-awareness! Students who can identify their strengths will be more likely to build on them to improve their areas of growth; they will probably have a greater motivation, and will be more self-confident. Here's a 3-step process to help students identify their strengths.

3. **Teach self-talk strategies to help students (re)focus.** Learning ways to cope with stress when faced with a difficult task (such as solving a complex problem) or strategies to re-engage with a task that requires perseverance are essential in the Common Core math classroom. What can students tell themselves when they get stuck? Have students brainstorm strategies and give them suggestions. Taking a deep breath, rereading the problem and finding what they know, or taking one step at a time, are a few strategies that can help students re-engage with the task. This is a great article that provides tips to help students overcome the "run" response in math. Developing mathematically proficient students requires that teachers develop students' social and emotional competencies alongside their mathematical knowledge. You can help students develop self-awareness by discussing their emotional reaction to the subject and helping them identify

their strengths; self-management can be supported by teaching self-talk strategies that students can use to re-engage with challenging problems. How are you connecting SEL with your math instruction? Please share in the comments below!

Originally published in Social Emotional Learning and the Common Core blog by Lorea Martinez, Ph.D.

> *In Mathematics, the Common Core standards reflect the view that learning is a social process, implicitly calling for teaching practices that leverage the power of group work and collaborative learning.*

7.3 Teaching SEL in ELA, History and Math

by Lorea Martinez, Ph.D.

In an earlier post, I described the 3 strategies to address SEL in the classroom that CASEL (2013) recommends. The third strategy encourages integrating SEL with academic content, which means that you connect the strategies and vocabulary of your SEL instruction with your subject matter. In *Perseverance in Solving Problems* we saw how you can do this connection in your math class. Today, let's look at other subjects and see ways in which SEL can be integrated with the academic curriculum.

- **English-Language Arts.** There are several ELA Common Core Standards naturally aligned with social and emotional skills. For example, those related to describing characters in a story (RL.3.3), describing how a particular story plot unfolds and how the characters respond or change overtime (RL.6.3) or how particular lines of dialogue or incidents in a story propel the action

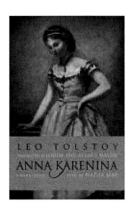

  (RL.8.3). When teaching these standards in the classroom, you will be helping students identify emotions (emotional literacy), analyzing the pros and cons of the characters' actions (consequential thinking), and identifying how emotions and actions are connected to motivation or long-term goals. In addition, research has shown (Kidd and Castano, 2013) that continued exposure to literary fiction could increase empathy.

My personal pick: Russian novels; exquisite in their description of complex characters and soul-searching processes!

- **History**. Teaching history offers a great opportunity for teachers and students to confront the complexities of humanity, in ways that promote critical thinking, empathy and moral development. The language provided by SEL around emotional literacy, self-management, social awareness and relationship building can help you create a safe environment for students to discuss subjects such as racism, immigration, diversity, human rights, etc. At the same time, historical figures can be analyzed through the lenses of social and emotional competencies. If you teach High School, you could use this lesson plan Nelson Mandela & The Fight Against Apartheid to analyze how Mandela used different social and emotional competencies through his fight against Apartheid. Also, Facing History and Ourselves has great resources for teachers (units, lessons plans, videos) to discuss complex moments in history and work with students to understand the range of human behavior.

- **Music.** The history of music is full of artists that struggled to find a place in the music scene, were often broke and sometimes lost hope that they would ever make it. Ask students about their favorite musicians and help them analyze these artists under the lens of social and emotional competencies. Another way to integrate SEL in your music class is analyzing songs through emotional literacy. I cannot think of a place where you can identify more emotions and feelings than in music (both with or without lyrics)! You can also discuss how music makes students feel and how different genres might generate similar/different emotions. Music is often therapeutic for a lot of us, try discussing with your students how music can be used to increase motivation or engage optimism!

In order to increase the impact of the SEL program in your class, you can integrate its content and language with the academic curriculum.

> *In order to increase the impact of the SEL program in your class, you can integrate its content and language with the academic curriculum.*

Addressing Common Core ELA standards related to characters and plots, analyzing historical figures through the lenses of social and emotional competencies or identifying the emotions and feelings that music generate are a few strategies that will develop students' social and emotional skills while they learn the specific academic content you 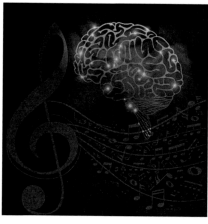 teach them in class. How do you integrate SEL with academic content? Please share!

Originally published in Social Emotional Learning and the Common Core blog by Lorea Martinez, Ph.D.

7.4 Integrating EQ with Academic Content in your classroom

Academic Standard	Write here an academic standard that your students need to master:
Lesson Plan/ Activities	Briefly describe one or two activities students will do to learn and apply the standard:
EQ Competencies	Thinking about the Six Seconds EQ model, identify the competencies students will need to put into practice to engage in the activities you described above. For example, students might need to navigate their emotions if they are presented with a challenging task.
Supporting your students' EQ	Write here one or two things you can do to support the EQ competencies that you identified as needed. For example, if you identified "navigate emotions" as a necessary skill, you might have students name their feelings about the challenging task and then brainstorm, as a group, strategies to manage these emotions before getting started.

> *Becoming an EQ Educator takes awareness, courage, and the belief that social and emotional learning is critical for students' success.*

8. Putting all the pieces together

Becoming an EQ Educator takes awareness, courage, and the belief that social emotional learning is critical for students' success. Your own practice of emotional intelligence can support you in the challenging and wonderful work of being an educator. When you build awareness and make intentional choices, you can increase empathy and make better decisions aligned with your purpose. We hope you've been inspired by this book and learned practical tools to assist you in your journey.

The Reflection part is up next. Now that you have read through these articles and posts, what's one idea you have found most useful for yourself? For students? For your practice, school, or university?

What is one personal take-away that you will start to apply right now?

How might this book be used in teaching at your school or institution?

And now, call to action! Reviewing the Benchmarks for Schools wishing to fully implement SEL (go back to page 40-45 if needed), what is one step you can take to move forward at your school in each of the three domains?

EQ Development for all:

EQ for the Classroom:

EQ for the School:

With whom will you talk to activate this plan?

For more information:

We wrote a peer-reviewed case study to illustrate how one school is working to fully implement EQ, using several of the Six Seconds tools that you have seen in this book. Here is the abstract:

In this case study, we examined how a school, committed to emotional intelligence (EQ) as a pillar, used assessment data to build positive school climate and strengthen the EQ of students and all community members. School leaders used multiple social-emotional and school climate assessments, over several years, to acquire data to enhance individual success, enrich classroom practice, and provide a strategy for schoolwide improvement. The school climate data, measuring trust, accountability, commitment, connection, and growth, became a roadmap for social, emotional, and academic learning to flourish. Teachers used data helped both youth and adults increase self-awareness, make better choices, and create a more supportive learning community. Teachers used assessment results to guide curriculum development and classroom management. Administrators examined their own effectiveness individually and as a team and planned teacher professional development and parent workshops. Emotions and cognition work together and, by assessing EQ as robustly as academic learning, educators at this school, committed to a holistic approach, are able to envision a path forward, individually and as a school community. A three-part framework for schoolwide implementation of social emotional learning is used to develop (a) student and adult competencies, (b) classroom practices, and (c) whole school approaches, including school climate and administrative team leadership.

The complete article can be found on Science Direct, which may require a university subscription.

www.sciencedirect.com/science/article/pii/S0193397316301034

Interested in finding out more about how EQ can support your work in schools?

www.6seconds.org/education/

At Six Seconds, we believe emotions are valuable signals that help us survive and thrive. When we learn how to use them, emotions help us make more effective decisions, connect with others, find and follow purpose — and lead a more whole-hearted life.